# Teaching Reading in the Middle Grades

Susan Abbott, M.A.

Teacher Created Materials, Inc.

Cover Design by Darlene Spivak

Copyright © 1999 Teacher Created Materials, Inc. All rights reserved.

No part of this publication may be reproduced in whole or in part, or stored in any retrieval system, or transmitted in any form or by any means, electronic, mechanical, photocopying, recording, or otherwise, without written permission from the publisher, Teacher Created Materials, Inc., 6421 Industry Way, Westminster, CA 92683.

Made in U.S.A.

ISBN 1-57690-474-1

Order Number TCM 2474

www.teachercreated.com

# Table of Contents

Introduction . . . . . . . . . . . . . . . . . . . . . . . . . . . . . . . . . . . . . . . . . . . . . . . . . . . . . . . . iv

Reading in the Middle Grades: An Overview . . . . . . . . . . . . . . . . . . . . . . . . . . . . . . . . . 1

What Every Teacher Should Know About Reading Instruction . . . . . . . . . . . . . . . . . . . . 9

Across the Curriculum: The Demands of Content Area Reading . . . . . . . . . . . . . . . . . . 30

Expanding Vocabulary and Conceptual Framework . . . . . . . . . . . . . . . . . . . . . . . . . . . 52

Using Content Literacy Strategies to Improve Comprehension . . . . . . . . . . . . . . . . . . . 68

Creating Readers: Motivating Students to Read! . . . . . . . . . . . . . . . . . . . . . . . . . . . . . 82

References . . . . . . . . . . . . . . . . . . . . . . . . . . . . . . . . . . . . . . . . . . . . . . . . . . . . . . . 90

# Introduction

The title for this Professional's Guide could easily be *Teaching Reading in the Middle Grades and Beyond!* The theory, concepts, and strategies found within are applicable to middle and junior high, high school, and even college level students.

Reading is a skill based subject with its own content and structure, yet it is also a process that underlies teaching and learning in every subject. Consequently, reading instruction must vary to accommodate purpose. Students need instruction to develop as independent and proficient readers, yet they also need instruction in strategies that are applicable to specific content areas.

*Teaching Reading in the Middle Grades* is designed to help classroom teachers and school administrators provide instruction that builds literacy skills by accommodating and supporting the reading needs and abilities of each student. This Professional's Guide looks at reading instruction as a threefold process: reading as a subject, reading as an integral part of content area instruction, and reading as a lifelong habit for information and entertainment.

# Reading in the Middle Grades: An Overview

Think about the characteristics that children share as they enter kindergarten: excitement, motivation, energy, and expectation! They are excited to learn, to share, to play, and most of all, to READ! Reading is almost magical to young children; they view it with awe and anticipation. Certainly one of the finest moments for any teacher is that point where a child amazingly states, "I can read!" Through third or fourth grade, educational practices reinforce this motivation to read by providing consistent, structured instruction and practice in the process and skills of reading. Abruptly, however, this instruction stops. Students are expected to read, and the business of teaching becomes content driven. For many students, the magic of reading turns to drudgery, becoming only a rote task. For those who are struggling, reading becomes a source of distress; they are placed in intervention programs, retained in a grade, or left alone to "catch up" or fail.

> **Certainly one of the finest moments for any teacher is that point where a child amazingly states, "I can read!"**

The reading ability of this nation's middle and secondary school students is currently a matter of great concern. Many states are in the process of setting rigorous grade level standards for students as well as requiring proof of reading instruction competency from their teachers. Why do so many children read below grade level? There is a never-ending cycle of blame: colleges and universities say, "if only the high school teachers did a better job;" high school teachers blame the middle school curriculum and instructional practices; in turn, those teachers say the responsibility rests with the elementary school; teachers blame parents; parents and employers blame the educational system.

Consider the following anecdote. At a recent gathering, the president of a local teacher's organization told the tale of three young men who walked the same route on their way to the bus stop. As the first man walked along the sidewalk, he tripped and fell into a rather large hole that had been created during road construction. He blamed the city and sued for damages. As the second man walked along the sidewalk, he tripped and fell into the same hole. He blamed himself for being so careless. As the third man walked along the sidewalk, he noticed a "Construction Ahead" caution sign. He decided to take another route.

**It is the responsibility of every teacher, every administrator, every parent, and every student to see to it that reading is a priority in the educational system.**

Rather than blame, it is far better to accept the responsibility and challenge of making every child a reader. To do so, educators need to heed the warning signs and "take another route." Reading is a process that grows and develops with use and practice. Reading instruction should never end; it belongs at every grade level, from kindergarten through freshman year in college. It is the responsibility of every teacher, every administrator, every parent, and every student to see to it that reading is a priority in the educational system.

Learning becomes increasingly complex as children enter middle grades, middle schools, and junior high classrooms. "For first-year students in middle school, change is pervasive. No longer does a student's day revolve around a single teacher. In middle school, kids have different classes and different teachers" (Love, 1998, p. B13). In addition, they have to meet the expectations of rigid academic standards. While educational standards vary from state to state, they do have one skill in common: the ability to read and make meaning from increasingly difficult subject matter materials. Examples of grade level reading expectations are provided in the chart on the following page.

| Grades Four and Five | Grades Six, Seven, and Eight |
|---|---|
| • Recognize main point, locate supporting details, write a summary, use reference materials, and cite sources correctly.<br>• Read and write numbers in the millions.<br>• Get meaning from text about algebra, geometry, history, and science.<br>• Use Latin and Greek word roots as a word recognition tool.<br>• Recognize fact and opinion. Draw inferences from text. Analyze characters; recognize plot. | • Read the periodic table of elements.<br>• Follow text organization patterns: sequence, cause and effect, comparison and contrast.<br>• Distinguish between connotative and denotative word usage.<br>• Write stories that develop a plot as well as character.<br>• Use proper grammar, punctuation, and sentence structure.<br>• Spell correctly.<br>• Locate, use and understand figurative language.<br>• Conduct research and write reports.<br>• Differentiate various genre. |

Grade Level Reading Expectations

## Reading Instruction in the Middle Grades: A Paradigm

Reading instruction must be an integral part of the instructional day for all middle and secondary grade students. The paradigm is this:

**Reading Instruction in the Middle Schools**

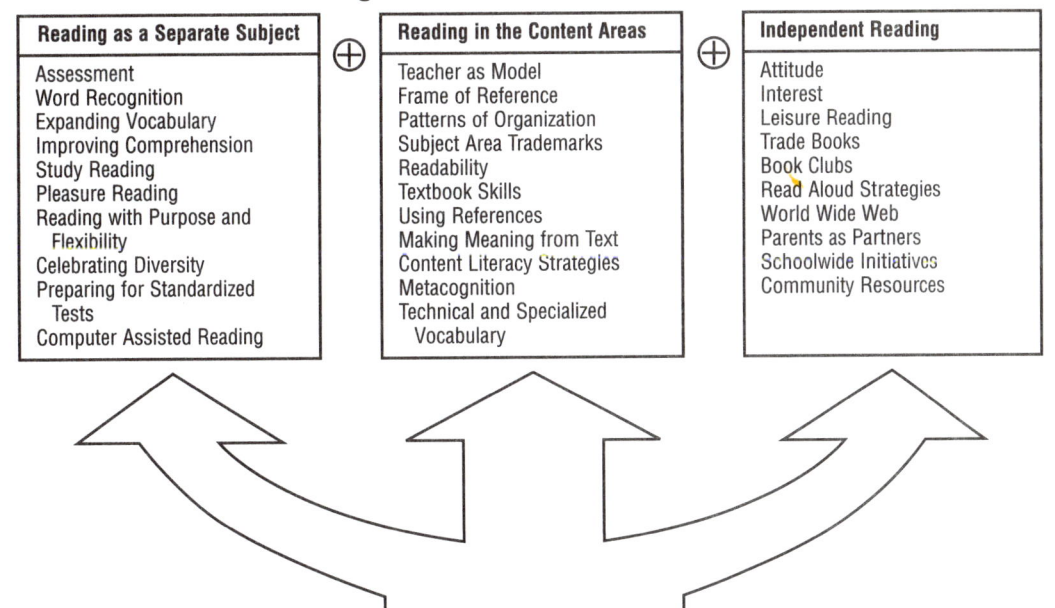

| Reading as a Separate Subject | Reading in the Content Areas | Independent Reading |
|---|---|---|
| Assessment<br>Word Recognition<br>Expanding Vocabulary<br>Improving Comprehension<br>Study Reading<br>Pleasure Reading<br>Reading with Purpose and Flexibility<br>Celebrating Diversity<br>Preparing for Standardized Tests<br>Computer Assisted Reading | Teacher as Model<br>Frame of Reference<br>Patterns of Organization<br>Subject Area Trademarks<br>Readability<br>Textbook Skills<br>Using References<br>Making Meaning from Text<br>Content Literacy Strategies<br>Metacognition<br>Technical and Specialized Vocabulary | Attitude<br>Interest<br>Leisure Reading<br>Trade Books<br>Book Clubs<br>Read Aloud Strategies<br>World Wide Web<br>Parents as Partners<br>Schoolwide Initiatives<br>Community Resources |

Reading as a Subject + Content Area Reading Skills + Independent Reading = **A Reader!**

### Teaching Reading as a Subject

In a recent editorial, Adrienne Mack states that plummeting high school reading scores should be no puzzle. "Even as employers' demand for higher literacy skills climbs, language arts remains tucked into a 55-minute period. Fifty-five minutes to teach literature, reading and writing. Add English language instruction to those same 55 minutes and you have a formula for plummeting test scores."

The skills involved in the reading process need to be studied and practiced by all students through the middle grades, high school years, and into college. Reading can be a separate class that each student takes as part of the daily schedule, or it can be included in English class. However, if the study of reading is attached to the English curriculum, it needs daily, allocated time, dedicated attention, and skilled teachers. Teaching reading is not the same as teaching literature! "Reading skills are important to the study of literature, as they are to the study of every content area. It should be understood, however, that teaching literature, even in junior high school, should not consist merely of having students read stories and then giving vocabulary drills and exercises to find details and main ideas" (Roe, 1991, p. 13).

If reading instruction becomes a separate and regular part of the daily schedule, caution should be taken so that students are not placed in classes based upon test scores or ability. Rather, every class should offer instruction for readers across a wide range of abilities. Intervention strategies for students who have severe reading problems should be individualized and offered as an adjunct—not a replacement to—regular studies. Reading should not be treated as a remedial subject; to do so places an almost insurmountable barrier of negativism. Students develop through their adolescent and teen years, and so does the reading process; all students benefit from reading instruction, and planned reading instruction is needed for each student at every grade level.

In the 1995 *Revised National Assessment of Educational Progress, Reading: A First Look,* P. L. Williams, C. M. Reese, J. R. Campbell, J. Mazzeo, and G. W. Phillips state that an eighth-grade student performing at the proficient level in reading should be able to demonstrate the following:

- overall understanding of reading in text
- comprehension of literal and inferential information
- extension of text ideas by drawing conclusions, making inferences

- connecting information gained from reading to experiential background as well as reading background
- processing information from reading and making corrections and additions to previously gained information

**Teaching Reading as an Integral Part of Each Content Area**

Many teachers believe that covering a subject area is their primary responsibility.

> *Subject matter has always dominated education. In elementary schools, the day is punctuated by shifts from reading to math to science to social studies, as students put away one set of books or papers and take out another. In middle schools and high schools, students move from class to class, subject to subject, without seeing how one subject relates to another. Even within subject areas, the layer-cake approach to curriculum obscures common ideas and themes, reinforcing the notion that subject-area knowledge consists of a set of discrete facts and theories"* (Badger, 1992, p. 1).

Do these comments sound familiar? "I don't have time to teach reading." "I have to cover all the chapters." "I have to cover all of the concepts." "Students should know how to read by middle school." "It's not my job to teach reading." These are all too familiar laments of subject area teachers. But, take a minute to think about the various meanings of cover—case, wrapper, and roof, to name a few. It is doubtful that any good teacher considers covering material the real goal of instruction, yet often curriculum is driven by quantity of material rather than quality of instruction. Reading instruction needs to be an integral part of every subject area. According to *Becoming a Nation of Readers*, it is the most logical place since reading strategies prove most useful when the "student is grappling with important but unfamiliar content" (Anderson, 1985). Reading instruction in a content area complements the learning process for that subject.

> *English classes shouldn't be the only place where youngsters learn reading and writing; such instruction should extend throughout the curriculum. Math teachers need to explain how to write out, in Standard English prose, a math problem and solution. Science teachers need to walk their students through the textbook examining pictures, explaining the function of figures and captions, bold headings and Italics. History teachers can provide instruction on reading charts and graphs, using the index to find specific information"* (Mack, 1998, p. B13).

**It is doubtful that any good teacher considers covering material the real goal of instruction, yet often curriculum is driven by quantity of material rather than quality of instruction.**

**Developing Independent Readers**

Nothing improves reading ability better than reading. Nothing improves critical thinking skills better than reading. Nothing improves writing ability better than reading. Literacy allows the opportunity of choice; a person who doesn't read or can't read must form opinions by relying on what others say. A person who can and does read has the power, ability, and resources to make informed, individual choices. Little, if anything, is more important to the future of the individual as well as the nation than the ability and motivation to read. The educational system must focus on the need for developing reading skills in each student in every classroom.

## Reading Concepts and Applications: Self-Assessment

A good starting point for this Professional's Guide is self-assessment. What do you know about reading concepts and their practical applications? Answer each of the following based on "working knowledge." In other words, do you know concept meanings and can you practically apply this knowledge in your everyday teaching. Use the following scale for your ratings:

1 = Strong knowledge of concept/use frequently
2 = Fair knowledge of concept/have some idea about classroom application
3 = Little knowledge of concept/have never tried or do not know how to apply in teaching
4 = Unfamiliar with concept

> *A person who can and does read has the power, ability, and resources to make informed, individual choices.*

| RATE YOUR ABILITY TO ASSESS OR INTERPRET THE FOLLOWING: |
|---|

_____1. Reading attitude and interests

_____2. Standardized reading test scores

_____3. Content reading skills

_____4. Content area learning styles

| RATE YOUR ABILITY TO CONSTRUCT AND USE EACH OF THE FOLLOWING: |
|---|

_____5. Authentic reading assessment strategies

_____6. Readability levels of texts/materials

_____7. Directed reading lessons: Pre/Adjunct/Post reading activities

_____8. Materials incorporating various levels of comprehension

| RATE YOUR ABILITY TO MEET INDIVIDUAL NEEDS... |
|---|

_____9. Plan and implement individualized reading instruction

_____10. Meet the reading needs of students from various ethnic, linguistic, cultural, and socioeconomic backgrounds

_____11. Develop student interest in reading as a leisure activity

_____12. Develop student interest/motivation in subject matter reading materials

_____13. Build positive student attitudes and self-esteem in reading, subject area, and learning in general

| RATE YOUR ABILITY TO TEACH EACH OF THE FOLLOWING: |
|---|

_____14. Technical, specialized, general vocabulary
_____15. Literal, interpretive, critical, and creative reading and thinking
_____16. Content area reading/study skills (SQ3R, mapping, etc.)
_____17. Reading skills specific to each subject area
_____18. Word recognition tactics
_____19. Reference skills

| RATE YOUR ABILITY TO FIND AND USE... |
|---|

_____20. Internet sites for teaching reading, motivating students to read, and finding reading resources
_____21. ERIC/Professional Journals
_____22. Resources for Computer Assisted Instruction in reading/content reading
_____23. Various materials at many grade levels to supplement textbooks

> Now, tabulate your results. First, add the number value of each response. Then, divide by 23.
> 
> Sum of responses ÷ # of responses (23) = Your starting point

**Analyze your Self-Assessment:**

1.0 = Strong knowledge of content reading fundamentals; use this text to locate resources and enhance your repertoire of content reading strategies.

2.0 = Good knowledge of content reading fundamentals; use this text to develop strategies for incorporating reading into your everyday teaching repertoire.

3.0 = The theories of content reading are somewhat familiar; use this text to increase your theoretical foundation and build a repertoire of teaching strategies

4.0 = The theories and strategies of content area reading are unfamiliar. Use this text to build a foundation in content reading and acquire new teaching strategies.

## Concluding Remarks

"Expanded reading and writing instruction acknowledges that literacy growth is continuous and does not stop at the end of fourth or sixth grade. Neither should instruction" (Ruddell, 1997, p. 13). Reading instruction is especially important in grades four through eight because it is during this time that students meet new subjects that require reading skills different than those taught in the first three grades. It is a period in which positive self-esteem is critical to success, and little damages self esteem more than the inability to read and the resulting cycle of academic failure.

> *Middle school and secondary reading and writing instruction provides for all students: those who are achieving satisfactorily, those who simply need more time to arrive at expected achievement levels, those who are in the process of becoming fluent and literate in a second language, and those whose achievement goes well beyond the norm (Ruddell, 1997, p. 13).*

Continue reading this Professional's Guide to explore the concepts mentioned in the "Self-Assessment." In addition, find practical suggestions, resources, and actual samples of instructional strategies. Finally, consider several theoretical foundations of reading instruction that will be presented in order to plan the best possible reading instructional program for students in middle and secondary grades.

**It is a period in which positive self-esteem is critical to success, and little damages self esteem more than the inability to read and the resulting cycle of academic failure.**

# What Every Teacher Should Know About Reading Instruction

## The Reading Process

Over the past twenty-five years, I have asked thousands of students and teachers to define reading. Whether arrived at individually or collaboratively, the answers have one thing in common—they are all different! The *Literacy Dictionary* explains the term reading by listing the evolution of process-oriented definitions from experts including Thorndike, Gray, Goodman, Durkin, and Spache (Harris & Hodges, 1995, p. 206). Reading is a complex process involving physiological, psychological, cognitive, and experiential factors. Perhaps the one word that appears most often in definitions of reading is "meaning." Readers make meaning from text. "Just as we use information stored in schemata to understand and interact with the world around us, so do we use this knowledge to make sense of print" (Ruddell, 1997, p. 23).

**Readers make meaning from text.**

## Measuring Reading Ability and Achievement

Public sentiment and political rhetoric focus on standardized testing as the means to measuring reading achievement and attainment of grade level standards, but misconceptions about such testing often lead to misuse. Standardized test scores give only a rough estimate of a student's performance. Listed below are several of the major cautions that must be employed when using and interpreting standardized reading tests.

**The professional judgment of the teacher, coupled with authentic measures, is a far better indicator of student achievement and potential than a standardized test.**

### CAUTION: STANDARDIZED TESTING

- A low score can damage an already fragile self-concept.
- A grade level equivalent score is a guess. It does not mean much. It does not mean that a child is performing at that particular grade level. It should never be given to students or parents. The International Reading Association has taken a firm position against the use of grade equivalent scores.
- Scores can easily overestimate or underestimate a student's actual reading ability. Just one right or wrong answer can make a big difference in a score. In addition, a score may lose validity at certain age levels or competence levels.
- Unless otherwise stated in the technical manual, test makers expect students to have a grade level mastery of the English Language.
- Knowledge of poor test scores can lower teacher and student expectations. It can crush enthusiasm and motivation for learning.
- The professional judgment of the teacher, coupled with authentic measures, is a far better indicator of student achievement and potential than a standardized test. Placement decisions should rest with the teacher or multiple measures, but never with a single standardized test score.
- The norm-referenced group (the population that sampled or tried the test) must match the population of the group that is taking the test. Otherwise, test bias becomes an issue.
- Beware of the Standard Error of Measurement (SEM); it is a powerful, yet little known concept. It is the "plus or minus" estimate of test error. On any day, on a particular test, the student's real, true score could be plus or minus either a number of points or a number of months. Either way, consequences can be devastating in issues of student placement or teacher retention.
- If the content of the test does not match the content of the curriculum, then the test will not fairly or accurately measure achievement.
- Comparable forms (for example, form A and form B) of the same test may not be parallel, thereby failing to show accurate gains or losses.
- The student's speed of work may affect the score as indicated by the slow, thorough, and accurate student who completes only a portion of the test and thereby gets a low score. Also, students who read English as a second language may be unfairly penalized by time restraints.
- Student guessing may unduly raise scores. Randomly filling in all of the blanks before time runs out will also affect the accuracy factor.
- An individual's performance differs from day to day because of extraneous causes (lack of sleep, sickness, hunger, etc.); it is also affected by environmental factors (large, noisy group setting, students who don't take the test seriously, etc.).
- The norms, content, and language of a standardized test become outdated very quickly. An outdated test is a sure way to raise the issue of bias.

There are several widely used test batteries that include sections designed to measure reading skills: California Achievement Test (CAT); Stanford Achievement Test (SAT); Texas Assessment of Academic Skills (TAAS); Comprehensive Test of Basic Skills (CTBS); Metropolitan Achievement Test (MAT); Iowa Test of Basic Skills (ITBS). Tables 1 and 2 offer an overview of the middle grade reading skills sampled by these major achievement batteries.

### Table 1: Content Analysis of MAT, SAT, and TAAS Middle School Level: Reading Achievement Section

| MAT (Fourth Edition) Grade 8 | SAT Grade 8 | TAAS Grade 7 |
|---|---|---|
| Vocabulary Skills<br>√ Synonyms/Antonyms<br>√ Multiple Meanings | Vocabulary<br>√ Word Meanings<br>√ Context Clues<br>√ Multiple Meanings | |
| Comprehension<br>√ Stories/Questions | Comprehension<br>√ Stories<br>√ Listening | Comprehension<br>√ Vocabulary<br>√ Supporting Ideas<br>√ Main Idea<br>√ Relationships/Outcomes<br>√ Generalizations<br>√ Inferences<br>√ Evaluation |

**Many batteries also include sections on study skills that rely heavily on reading.**

### Table 2: Content Analysis of CAT, CTBS, and ITBS Middle School Level: Reading Achievement Section

| CAT (Fourth Edition) Grade 8 | CTBS (Revised) Grade 8 | ITBS (Fourth Edition) Grade 8 |
|---|---|---|
| Vocabulary<br>√ Synonyms/Antonyms<br>√ Words in Context<br>√ Derivations | Vocabulary<br>√ Synonyms/Antonyms<br>√ Words in Context<br>√ Derivations<br>√ Affix Meanings<br>√ Multiple Meanings | Vocabulary<br>√ Vocabulary Skills |
| Comprehension<br>√ Passages/Questions | Comprehension<br>√ Selections<br>√ Critical Reading | Comprehension<br>√ Selections/Questions |

Many batteries also include sections on study skills that rely heavily on reading. These skills include using parts of a textbook, finding information in an index, dictionary skills, using reference sources, and writing a summary or outline.

Many schools use standardized reading tests along with or instead of achievement batteries. The most commonly used include the following:

| TEST | PUBLISHER | ADDRESS |
| --- | --- | --- |
| Nelson Denny Reading Test | The Riverside Publishing Company | 8420 Bryn Mawr Ave. Chicago, IL 60631 |
| Gates-MacGinitie Reading Tests | The Riverside Publishing Company | 8420 Bryn Mawr Ave. Chicago, IL 60631 |
| Degrees of Reading Power (DRP) | Touchstone Applied Science Associates, Inc. | Fields Lane P.O. Box 382 Brewster, NY 10509-0382 |
| Stanford Diagnostic Reading Test, Fourth Edition (SDRT4) | Psychological Corporation | 555 Academic Court San Antonio, TX 78204-2498 |

**Grade equivalent scores or percentile rankings should not be viewed as the sole or best source of information.**

For specific information and a critique about any test in print, consult *Tests in Print and Mental Measurements Yearbook,* references from the Buros Institute of Mental Measurements. The Web site location for the Buros Institute is

> www.unl.edu/buros

## Interpretation of Test Scores

Grade equivalent scores or percentile rankings should not be viewed as the sole or best source of information. Rather, a teacher should look at the number of items the student attempted on each section and the number of those attempted that are correct. This is the accuracy factor. Most important, the teacher should look at patterns, or score relationships. Look at the example of Jenny, a sixth grade student, and the scores she received on a standardized reading test.

> Vocabulary         Raw Score 32
>
> Comprehension      Raw Score 15
>
> Rate 17 (number attempted on comprehension section)
> * The number possible in each section is 48.

If reported as a percentile or grade equivalent, Jenny's score on the comprehension section would be dismal. However, look at the pattern chart below for a different perspective of Jenny's comprehension.

| Grade Level | Vocabulary | Comprehension | Rate |
|---|---|---|---|
| 12 | | | |
| 11 | | | |
| 10 | | | |
| 9 | | | |
| 8 | | | |
| 7 | | | |
| 6 | | | |
| 5 | | | |
| 4 | | | |
| 3 | | | |
| 2 | | | |
| 1 | | | |

Jenny's problem may just be one of rate; she reads slowly, but she is accurate. Is she struggling to comprehend, or is there some other factor that is interfering? Her word knowledge is good, so her potential to comprehend is excellent. Authentic assessment can help the teacher determine why Jenny is reading so slowly:

- Does she have a vision problem? Does she wear glasses? Did she wear them for the test?
- Does she lose her place? Does she make repeated regressions?
- Does her attention wander?
- Does she have difficulty making the transition from oral reading to silent reading?
- Is English her second language? If so, does she need extra time to translate?

Only after analyzing the score relationships and accuracy factor can the teacher make valid interpretations.

## Authentic Assessment

Alvermann and Phelps state that "students should receive instruction based on their capabilities, not their weaknesses. In order to plan effective instruction, we need to learn as much as we can about students' norms, values, traditions, language, and beliefs, as well as their reading, writing, and study skills" (1998, p. 106). The purpose of authentic assessment should be to find out what students can do as well as what they like to do! Authentic strategies that work well for assessment of reading and content reading ability include the following:

✓ Attitude Scale    ✓ Learning Styles Inventory    ✓ Kidwatching
✓ Interest Survey   ✓ Content Reading Sampler
✓ Cloze             ✓ Text Response/Retelling

> **The purpose of authentic assessment should be to find out what students can do as well as what they like to do!**

## Attitudes, Self-Perceptions, Interests, and Learning Styles

Attitude determines whether or not a student will approach a situation with positive feelings or try to avoid it because of negative feelings. Student attitudes about reading and other subjects are formed through cultural, school, and social experiences; by middle school, attitudes can be quite set. Students often come to a new class with firmly rooted ideas about their likes, dislikes, and abilities. "I can't do math! I am a bad reader! History books are boring!"

"Reading attitude….consists of three components; a *cognitive* component (one's beliefs or opinions about reading), an *affective component* (one's evaluations of or feelings about reading), and a *behavioral component* (one's intentions to read and actual reading behavior)" (Vacca, 1996, p. 388). A reading attitude scale can be used to measure how the student feels about reading. An attitude scale can also be content specific, i.e., measuring how the student feels about social studies, science, etc. It can be given as a pre/post measure to determine whether or not a program or course has created a positive change in student attitude. Two samples of attitude scales are given on the next few pages. The first, Reading Attitude Survey, measures a student's perceptions about reading in general; the second measures reading as well as subject matter attitude in the content area of social studies.

## Identifying Interests and Learning Styles

Reading and content interests go hand in hand with student attitudes. "Students' interests and self-concepts are interwoven into the fabric of reading attitude. What students like to read—their interests—influence when they read, why they read, and how often they read" (Vacca, 1996, p. 388). It is vital that content area teachers know what students like to read, what their hobbies are, and what their general likes/dislikes are so they can plan curriculum accordingly.

A learning style is the way in which a learner best receives information. Does the student see and remember, hear and remember, learn through movement, learn by touching, or learn best in some combination of these modalities? The learning style of a student can vary from subject to subject; a student who can curl up on a chair and digest a work of fiction may, in fact, need to "do" math. It is important for teachers to be aware of student learning styles so curriculum and activities can be planned accordingly.

A simple way to explore student learning styles is to use a survey. Following are extracts from interest/learning styles surveys for reading, physical education, foreign language, and social studies:

---

**Student attitudes about reading and other subjects are formed through cultural, school, and social experiences; by middle school, attitudes can be quite set.**

# Social Studies Attitude

**Directions:** After reading each statement, select a numeric value (1-4) which best reflects your response to the question. There are no right or wrong answers so just mark what you think.

1. _____ Studying history is fun.
2. _____ I like learning about other cultures.
3. _____ Maps and graphs can be useful in everyday life.
4. _____ If I had the opportunity, I would like to visit a museum.
5. _____ I like to learn about people from the past.
6. _____ I find it easy to relate to historical people and events.
7. _____ I am good at social studies.
8. _____ If I had the chance, I would like to visit other countries.
9. _____ Reading from a history book is enjoyable.
10. _____ Learning about the past is important.
11. _____ I would like to read magazine articles about history and geography.
12. _____ I would like to continue studying about history and geography in future years.

1 = Strongly Disagree
2 = Disagree
3 = Agree
4 = Strongly Agree

## Attitude Scoring Information

The numerical scoring value of each question corresponds to the response value given by the student. For example, a "strongly agree" response is worth 4 points, while a "strongly disagree" is worth 1 point. Add up the total for responses to questions 1–12. After calculating the total, look at the chart below to determine the student's current attitude toward social studies.

| Total Points | Attitude Group |
|---|---|
| 40-48 | Very positive attitude |
| 30-39 | Positive attitude |
| 20-29 | Somewhat negative attitude |
| 12-20 | Negative attitude |

# Reading Attitude Survey

| Directions: This survey asks how you feel about reading and books. This survey is not a test, and it will not affect your grade. It will be used to help plan class activities and instruction. Answer as honestly as you can by checking the column that indicates how you feel about each statement.<br><br>SA = Strongly Agree    A = Agree<br>SD = Strongly Disagree    D = Disagree | SA | A | D | SD |
|---|---|---|---|---|
| 1. Books are boring. | | | | |
| 2. Reading is a waste of time. | | | | |
| 3. I love to read. | | | | |
| 4. I think I am a good reader. | | | | |
| 5. I enjoy going to the bookstore or library to get a new book. | | | | |
| 6. I don't read anything but homework assignments and only those if I must! | | | | |
| 7. I think that I am a poor reader. | | | | |
| 8. I don't like most of the books in school. | | | | |
| 9. I like to read in class. | | | | |
| 10. I like to read for pleasure every day. | | | | |
| 11. Reading gets boring after about ten minutes. | | | | |
| 12. I don't learn much from reading. | | | | |
| 13. I would rather read than watch TV. | | | | |

**Scoring:** *The positive items are: 3, 4, 5, 9, 10, 13*

    Give four points for SA, three points for A, two points for D, and one point for SD.

*The negative items are: 1,2,6,7,8,11,12*

    Give four points for SD, three for D, two for A, and one for SA.

**Add:** Positive Items _____ + Negative Items_____

                  Total: _____

**RATE YOUR ATTITUDE:**
Very Positive          = 45–52
Positive                 = 39–44
Somewhat Positive  = 28–38
Neutral                 = 26–27
Negative              = 14–25
Very Negative       = 13 and below

## Reading Interest/Learning Styles Survey

1. Do you like to read for pleasure? Why or Why not?
2. What is the title of your favorite book?
 Why is it your favorite?
3. When you have free time, what do you like to do?
4. Place a √ by the types/subjects of reading that you like best:

    ___Magazines        ___Biography        ___War
    ___Poetry           ___Health/Exercise  ___Science Fiction
    ___Mystery          ___Computers        ___Plays
    ___Art              ___Real Life        ___Animals
    ___Music            ___Sports           ___Cars
    ___Rock Stars       ___Astrology        ___Supernatural
    ___Games            ___Romance          ___Humor/Jokes
    ___Cartoons         ___Other:_____

If given the choice, you would rather . . .
_____read the book by yourself
_____watch the movie
_____listen to someone else read the book
_____participate in a read-around, with everyone taking turns reading the book
_____get someone else to read the book for you and tell you what it is about!

## Physical Education Interest/Learning Styles Survey

1. What did you like about physical education last year?
2. What did you dislike about physical education last year?
3. Listed below are several activities. Place a (√) next to the activities in which you most prefer to participate. Place a ( - ) next to the activities in which you would rather not participate. If undecided, leave the space blank.

    _____Gymnastics             _____Softball
    _____Flag Football          _____Baseball
    _____Physical Fitness Tests _____Soccer
    _____Basketball             _____Aerobics
    _____Golf                   _____Volleyball
    _____Swimming/Diving        _____Track and Field
    _____Other (describe) _____

4. Do you like to read about athletes and sports? Why or why not?

Place a √ by any of the activities that you would like to do:

_____Play indoor sports (volleyball, aerobics, weight training, etc.)
_____Watch a video about a sport or sporting event
_____Listen to a lecture and take notes about game rules and strategies
_____Read a biography about a famous athlete
_____Play outdoor sports (football, baseball, etc.)
_____Play competitive, team sports
_____Play competitive, individual sports
_____Watch a skill demonstration (How to…)
_____Teach others how do to a skill
_____Watch a school or professional sporting event
_____Read the Sports Section of the daily newspaper

## Spanish 1 Interest/Learning Styles Survey

Directions: Please answer each question as completely and accurately as possible.
1. Why do you want to study and learn Spanish?
2. Do you enjoy reading about new cultures? Please explain.
3. Would you like to travel to another country? If so, where would you like to visit?

Directions: Please rank the following groups of items in order of what you would most like to do in Spanish class to what you would least like to do.
1. Work with a partner in pronunciation of Spanish words.
2. Listen to a tape recording of native Spanish speakers.
3. Use a Spanish dictionary and write out definitions for vocabulary.
4. Participate in a group discussion about vocabulary meanings.

Ranking: 1st Favorite_____      3rd Favorite_____
         2nd Favorite_____      4th Favorite_____

Directions: Please place a √ next to the following activities you would like to do:
_____Learn a new language
_____See videos about new cultures
_____Listen to a language other than English
_____Work with a small group to complete class projects
_____Go on a field trip
_____Answer questions from the textbook
_____Read about new people and places
_____Learn new vocabulary words

## History Interest/Learning Styles Survey

1. History could be more interesting if… _____
_____

2. If I could live during any other year, it would be…Why? _____
_____

3. The three activities I like the most are…

    1. _____
    2. _____
    3. _____

4. What historical figure would you like to meet? Why?

5. I enjoy reading about… _____
_____

When preparing for a quiz, I like to…
    _____study by myself              _____study with the whole class
    _____study with a partner         _____study with a tutor

When learning something new, I prefer to…
    _____watch a video about it              _____act it out
    _____listen to the teacher talk about it _____write about it
    _____read about it

## Kidwatching (Goodman, 1985)

In *Professional's Guide: Authentic Assessment* (1994), author Concetta Doti Ryan states that "observations should be planned and key on a particular area of learning…observations of students should take place in authentic situations with students doing authentic activities." Following are several examples of authentic assessment forms that can be used for reading.

Literacy Development Evaluation

### Language Arts Development Checklist (cont.)

| Skill | Quarter | | | |
|---|---|---|---|---|
| **Reading Development** | 1 | 2 | 3 | 4 |
| Uses picture cues | | | | |
| Uses context to identify meaning | | | | |
| Makes meaningful substitutions | | | | |
| Recognizes language patterns | | | | |
| Reads for sustained period | | | | |
| Reads for pleasure | | | | |
| Reads for information | | | | |
| Reads for research | | | | |
| Reads orally with expression | | | | |
| Monitors reading and self-corrects | | | | |
| Makes and confirms predictions | | | | |
| Selects appropriate reading material | | | | |
| Reads a variety of materials | | | | |
| Checks books out of school library | | | | |
| Checks books out of public library | | | | |
| **Literature Response** | 1 | 2 | 3 | 4 |
| Retells story | | | | |
| Summarizes story | | | | |
| Sequences story events accurately | | | | |
| Relates reading to personal experience | | | | |
| Awareness of story elements: | | | | |
|     setting | | | | |
|     characters | | | | |
|     plot | | | | |
|     theme | | | | |
|     mood | | | | |
| Discusses story with others | | | | |
| Gives supported opinion about the story | | | | |
| Extends reading through related projects | | | | |
| Discusses meaning of stories | | | | |
| Draws conclusions about story | | | | |
| Distinguishes fact from fiction | | | | |
| Compares and contrasts characters | | | | |
| Refers to text to support statements | | | | |
| Writes effective responses to literature | | | | |

*Reprinted from TCM 781 Language Arts Assessment, Teacher Created Materials, Inc., 1994.*

Anecdotal Records and Observations

# Triad Reading Evaluation

Name _____ Age _____
Grade _____ Date _____

|  | Teacher Comment | Student Comment | Parent Comment |
|---|---|---|---|
| Selects books to read | | | |
| Reads independently | | | |
| Reads at home | | | |
| Enjoys reading | | | |
| Understands what is read | | | |
| Reads a variety of material | | | |
| Enjoys listening to stories | | | |
| Reflects on reading | | | |

Reading goals for the year: _____

_Reprinted from TCM 781 Language Arts Assessment, Teacher Created Materials, Inc., 1994._

## Text Response/Retelling/Summary: Oral or Written

Use a rubric to assess comprehension after a student has read a story. Immediately following the reading of the story, ask the student to retell the story. The student's response is then scored against the reading comprehension rubric.

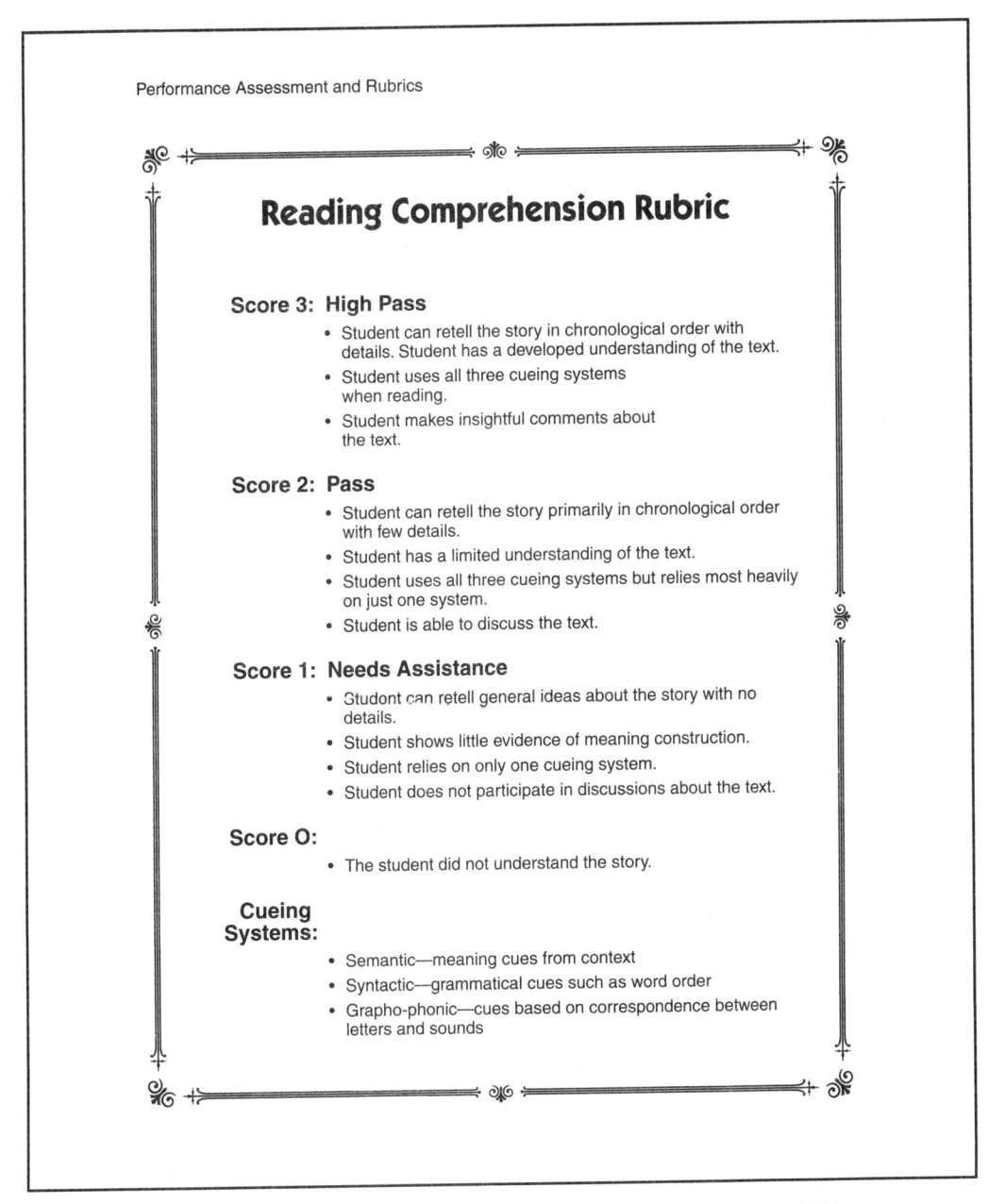

Performance Assessment and Rubrics

# Reading Comprehension Rubric

### Score 3: High Pass
- Student can retell the story in chronological order with details. Student has a developed understanding of the text.
- Student uses all three cueing systems when reading.
- Student makes insightful comments about the text.

### Score 2: Pass
- Student can retell the story primarily in chronological order with few details.
- Student has a limited understanding of the text.
- Student uses all three cueing systems but relies most heavily on just one system.
- Student is able to discuss the text.

### Score 1: Needs Assistance
- Student can retell general ideas about the story with no details.
- Student shows little evidence of meaning construction.
- Student relies on only one cueing system.
- Student does not participate in discussions about the text.

### Score 0:
- The student did not understand the story.

### Cueing Systems:
- Semantic—meaning cues from context
- Syntactic—grammatical cues such as word order
- Grapho-phonic—cues based on correspondence between letters and sounds

*Reprinted from TCM 781 Language Arts Assessment, Teacher Created Materials, Inc., 1994*

## Cloze (Taylor, 1953)

Cloze gives an estimate of a student's ability to use a particular textbook or piece of text. A teacher "whose goal is to teach a student rather than a textbook wants first to determine the student's ability to handle a given textbook" (Thelen, 1976, p. 6). It can also provide an indirect measure of a student's frame of reference about a given subject.

Here Is How Cloze Works:

1. Choose a reading passage of 250–300 words from text that students have not yet read but that you plan to assign (textbook passage, newspaper or magazine article, short story, novel, etc).
2. Leave the first sentence intact. Then, starting with the second sentence, delete every fifth word until fifty words have been deleted. Finish the sentence that contains the last deletion. Then, word process one more sentence, entirely intact.
3. For each deletion, leave a uniform-sized blank space.

> **Cloze gives an estimate of a student's ability to use a particular textbook or piece of text.**

### Sample Portion of Cloze

Surpluses have always been important to human communities. In prehistoric times, they __(1)__ people to survive hard __(2)__ or blazing summers when __(3)__ was scarce. With surpluses, __(4)__ groups of people could __(5)__ together, because there was __(6)__ food for everyone. Surpluses __(7)__ made it possible for __(8)__ to specialize, since not __(9)__ had to spend the __(10)__ hunting or gathering food. __(11)__, surpluses led to trade. __(12)__ one group had extra __(13)__ or grain on hand, __(14)__ would try to exchange __(15)__ for something else they __(16)__ —tools, seeds, or animal __(17)__.

From the beginning of __(18)__, people have had to __(19)__ what to do with __(20)__. The United States is __(21)__ faced with this decision __(22)__. This is a fertile __(23)__ wealthy nation, and it __(24)__ produces more than enough __(25)__ for its own people.

*Excerpt from A Message of Ancient Days, Houghton Mifflin Social Studies, 1991, page 142.*

Answers:

| 1. allowed | 6. enough | 11. Finally | 16. needed | 21. frequently |
|---|---|---|---|---|
| 2. winters | 7. also | 12. When | 17. skins | 22. today |
| 3. food | 8. people | 13. meat | 18. civilization | 23. and |
| 4. large | 9. everyone | 14. they | 19. decide | 24. often |
| 5. live | 10. day | 15. it | 20. surpluses | 25. food |

4. Administer to students after giving these directions as well as modeling a sample on the board:

   *Complete each blank with the word that you think the author used. You will have as much time as you need to work on this.*

Cloze Scoring:
1. Count the number of **exact** matches. Do not count synonyms even though they are ever so close in meaning. This may seem harsh, but the scoring range is wide, with a built-in margin of error. To accept synonyms would affect the reliability of the standard.
2. Multiply the total number of answers the student has correct by 2 to determine the percentage score. (In the case of the sample above, the score would be multiplied by 4 since this sample only contains 25 deletions).

Interpreting the Cloze Percentage:
1. *Independent Level:* A score of 60 percent or above indicates that the student is able to competently read the text or material.
2. *Instructional Level:* A score between 40–60 percent indicates that the student will need directed reading strategies and instructional guidance to comprehend the reading material with accuracy.
3. *Frustration Level*: A score below 40 percent indicates the text is difficult for the student. Ample guided reading instruction will be necessary.

## Content Reading Sampler

The Content Reading Sampler is an informal inventory designed to measure student background knowledge, conceptual readiness, and facility with text in a specific subject area. Students aren't necessarily good or poor readers across the curriculum. Rather, they often have strengths or weaknesses in a particular subject. This is especially true in the middle grades, where students meet new subjects for which they have little frame of reference.

A sampler should be designed to represent the skills and prerequisite knowledge a student needs to have about a subject at the beginning of instruction—in order to have the best chance of success in that subject. If a textbook will be used to teach the course content, possible topics for a Content Sampler include the following:

> **The Content Reading Sampler is an informal inventory designed to measure student background knowledge, conceptual readiness, and facility with text in a specific subject area.**

| Comprehension Skills |

- Locate topic
- Locate specific information
- Write the main idea
- Follow text organization
- Draw conclusions/make inferences
- Apply information to create new ideas
- Write a summary

### Vocabulary Knowledge

- Recognize and explain prerequisite specialized and technical vocabulary
- Use a variety of word attack skills
- Recognize relationship between vocabulary and key concepts

### Academic Reading Skills

- Organize material through outlining
- Concentrate while reading
- Set purpose for reading
- Adjust rate to purpose
- Employ academic reading techniques

### Using Textbook Parts

- Follow written directions
- Read and interpret graphs, charts, maps, illustrations
- Use book parts effectively: index, table of contents, textual aids

If the subject that is being sampled has an activity base rather than a textbook base, try the skill-based assessment such as the sample that begins on the following page. It is designed to provide information about experiential background, knowledge of content vocabulary, ability to understand content specific passages, and drawing skill. A Physical Education sampler might include a skill section related to reading a "how to" article and then trying to demonstrate the skill. In a technology class, students might be asked to follow the directions in a manual to repair or build an object.

# Content Reading Sampler
Intended for
Beginning Art Classes
Grades 7–9

## Part I—Vocabulary
Directions: Select from the numbered statements the best answer for the words below. Place the number in the place provided beside the lettered word.

1. an opening in a wall to let people or light pass through
2. when all parts of a work of art seem equal
3. a design made from a person's initials
4. the way of drawing that shows how shapes look in the distance
5. changing parts of things to make them look unreal
6. a shape or color that has a special meaning
7. when all parts of a work of art seem as though they belong together
8. the special way each artist does his or her work
9. a style of architecture with rounded arches
10. the inside and outside edges of any change of shape in an object
11. richly decorative art work that came after the Renaissance
12. a term which describes things that are different from each other
13. making something with imagination

ABSTRACT ___   SYMBOL ___   PERSPECTIVE ___

contour ___   ARCH ___   Style ___

Romanesque ___   MONOGRAM ___

conTRAST ___   BALANCE ___   BAROQUE ___

CREATIVE ___   UNITY ___

25

## Part II—Comprehension

Directions: Read the paragraph below. Follow the instructions given and make your list on the lines provided.

You know the buildings in your community—your home, the churches, service stations, supermarkets, stores, restaurants, movie theaters, and schools. Think of the kinds of buildings and what they look like. Family homes have many shapes, but most of them are the same size. A block of apartments is much bigger and usually built with several floors. Some apartments are tall towers.

Churches are very different from places where people live. They are larger and have simple shapes and large windows. They often have square towers and pointed spires. Motels, restaurants, supermarkets and other stores are usually low with plenty of parking. And you know what your school looks like.

Think of the buildings in your neighborhood. How well do you really know them? Can you describe how they look? Here is a chance to test your visual memory.

Pick out one building you know well. Write the name of the building on the top line. Then write down all the things you can remember about it. As you make your list describe the features so others can identify what type of building you are describing.

_____

_____

_____

_____

_____

_____

_____

## Part III—Skill

Directions: With your pencil, draw the building you described. Have your drawing fill the page. Look at your description to help you remember everything about it. When you finish add color to your drawing with the crayons on the table.

## Method of Scoring Content Sampler

1. Vocabulary—The numbers from 1 to 4 will indicate the number correct. 1 point for each three correct answers. There are a "baker's dozen" vocabulary words. The type of printing of each word gives a clue to the answer.

2. Comprehension—scored from 1 to 4 for things remembered

    1 point for the name of the building described on the correct line

    1 point for five things listed about the building being described

    1 point for ten or more things listed about the building described

    1 point if descriptive works were used in the list, e.g., pointed roof, red and green sign, etc.

3. Skill—scored from 1 to 4 points

    1 point—a background and foreground (Is everything on the same visual line?)

    1 point—everything included that was on the description

    1 point—Was anything added that wasn't on the list? (As the student drew did his or her mind's eye add more detail?)

    1 point—Was color added to the drawing? If not, was shading used effectively to add contrast and dimension to the drawing?

4. Total—The total points out of 12 possible will indicate the student's previous knowledge and exposure to art.

| Name of Student | (4) Vocabulary | | | | (4) Comprehension | | | | (4) Skill | | | | (12) Total |
|---|---|---|---|---|---|---|---|---|---|---|---|---|---|
| | 1 | 2 | 3 | 4 | 1 | 2 | 3 | 4 | 1 | 2 | 3 | 4 | |
| Jane Smith | | | X | | | | | X | | | X | | |
| Juan Garcia | X | | | | X | | | | | | X | | |
| | | | | | | | | | | | | | |
| | | | | | | | | | | | | | |
| | | | | | | | | | | | | | |
| | | | | | | | | | | | | | |
| | | | | | | | | | | | | | |
| | | | | | | | | | | | | | |

11–12 points—Independent—good exposure

8–10 points—Instructional—some exposure

6–8 points—Special help needed—little exposure

*below 6—Check with counselor or special teacher—no exposure or other problem

## Diversity: Factors That Affect Reading Achievement

I asked a class of my university students to "brainstorm" this topic: *What are the factors that influence reading achievement?* What started as a typical list suddenly and dramatically changed into an exciting discussion when someone shouted, DIVERSITY! Reflect upon the Diversity Web below; the concept of diversity encompasses all the characteristics that affect reading ability and achievement. Harold and Joan Herber consider diversity an instructional resource and offer this advice: "use the diversity among individuals that comprise the category of students so that both the category and the individuals are changed by the interaction. The spirit and gestalt of a class taught in this manner serve to illustrate the principle that the whole is *greater than* the sum of its parts" (Herber & Herber, 1993, p. 34).

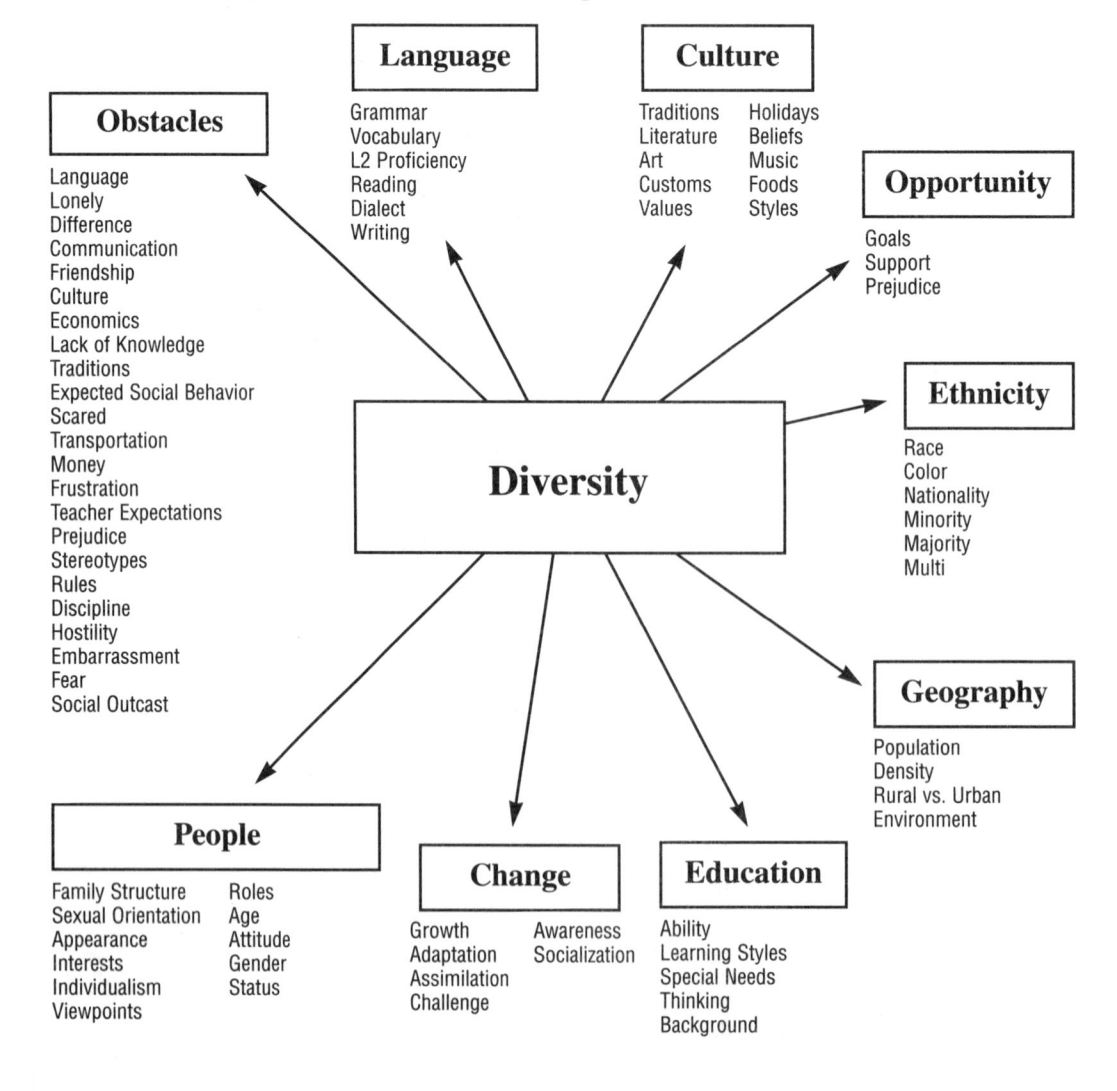

**Language**
Grammar
Vocabulary
L2 Proficiency
Reading
Dialect
Writing

**Culture**
Traditions   Holidays
Literature   Beliefs
Art          Music
Customs      Foods
Values       Styles

**Obstacles**
Language
Lonely
Difference
Communication
Friendship
Culture
Economics
Lack of Knowledge
Traditions
Expected Social Behavior
Scared
Transportation
Money
Frustration
Teacher Expectations
Prejudice
Stereotypes
Rules
Discipline
Hostility
Embarrassment
Fear
Social Outcast

**Opportunity**
Goals
Support
Prejudice

**Diversity**

**Ethnicity**
Race
Color
Nationality
Minority
Majority
Multi

**Geography**
Population
Density
Rural vs. Urban
Environment

**People**
Family Structure   Roles
Sexual Orientation Age
Appearance         Attitude
Interests          Gender
Individualism      Status
Viewpoints

**Change**
Growth       Awareness
Adaptation   Socialization
Assimilation
Challenge

**Education**
Ability
Learning Styles
Special Needs
Thinking
Background

## Concluding Remarks

This chapter has offered a glimpse of three major components of reading instruction: the process of reading, the assessment of reading ability, and the factors that affect reading achievement. It is important to understand that the process of reading is meaning driven—that students make meaning from text, they don't get meaning. Good readers activate schemata, set purposes for reading, constantly monitor their own comprehension, and stop to use a correction strategy when meaning isn't clear.

Equally important is the measurement of reading ability and achievement. Teachers should use caution when interpreting and reporting standardized reading test results. Scores are often misused, and the consequences can be disastrous. It is vital that authentic assessment measures hold equal weight in the student evaluation process; in fact, results of authentic assessment should take precedence over standardized test scores.

Finally, it is important to understand that the factors that most affect reading achievement are the characteristics that make each individual unique.

> *Expanded reading and writing instruction provides for diversity of student literacy abilities and needs. Middle school and secondary classrooms are filled with students who represent wide variation in literacy achievement and English language fluency. This diversity in no way suggests that there is anything "wrong" with any students or casts aspersions on students' previous classroom learning or life experience; nor does it mean that only the bilinguual/bicultural students require assistance with English-language fluency and literacy. Rather it recognizes and celebrates human differences (Ruddell, 1997, p. 13).*

**It is important to understand that the process of reading is meaning driven—that students make meaning from text, they don't get meaning.**

# Across the Curriculum: The Demands of Content Area Reading

**Content literacy is the ability to use reading and writing for the acquisition of new content in a given discipline.**

Content literacy is the ability to use reading and writing for the acquisition of new content in a given discipline. It is not the same as content knowledge; rather, it represents the skills needed to acquire knowledge of content (McKenna & Robinson, 1990, p. 9). Each subject area uses the English language in a unique way: common words exhibit a variety of meanings; patterns of text organization vary; connotative and figurative language subtly alter text. As a result, new types of reading skills are necessary. In order to learn successfully with texts, students must be exposed to a variety of reading and learning strategies that will help them meet the demands of coping with the new vocabulary, concepts, and text organization they will encounter.

## Reading skills common to all disciplines include the following:

- *Comprehension:* active learning in a content area is directly related to a student's ability to read, understand, and apply knowledge.
- *Vocabulary:* students need word recognition skills and vocabulary building techniques to tackle specialized word usage as well as technical words...both specialized usage and technical words.
- *Critical reading:* students must be able to find facts, make inferences, recognize fact from opinion, form judgments, consider bias, question source, and make generalizations.
- *Textbook skills:* students need to know how to use their texts—an index, a glossary, and internal textual aids such as contextual clues, bold print, subheadings, and cues.
- *Library tools and Internet:* students need to know how to effectively use these for research in a specific subject
- *Following directions:* students must follow sequence and use steps to solve a problem or create a product.
- *Study skills:* students need to read for purposes of summary writing and outlining, note taking, and finding information for test taking.

In addition to sharing these common reading skills, each content area presents its own, unique reading demands that students must learn to use and interpret. On the next several pages, reading skills specific to various subject areas are presented. Applications for teaching these skills follow.

### ART

1. Analyze and critique various art forms and objects.
2. Interpret abbreviations and graphic materials.
3. Study and internalize concepts and theories of technique, schools, historical principles, and practices.

An example of reading in the content area of art can be found on the next page.

# Reading in the Content Areas: Art

*Leonardo da Vinci* _____ *Renaissance and Baroque Artists*

# Extensions

1. According to the author of *The Annotated Mona Lisa* (see listing below), the definition of a *Renaissance man* is "...an omnitalented individual who radiates wisdom." Have students explain why Leonardo da Vinci was a good example of a Renaissance man.

2. While Leonardo was in Milan, he built a 22-foot (6.6 m) clay model of the duke's horse. Ultimately, it was to have been cast in bronze but war broke out and the bronze had to be used for weapons. Assign a group of students to find out who was involved in the war, the war's causes, and what became of the huge statue. Have them present their findings to the rest of the class.

3. Although da Vinci could write and draw with either hand, he preferred to use his left hand. Wherever he went he had a notebook in his pocket and kept sketches and notes about people, buildings, animals, plants, and designs. All of the writing was done in mirror writing which read from right to left. Give students an opportunity to simulate Leonardo's genius with either of these two activities.

    ✦ Instruct students to carry a small notebook with them at all times for a period of five school days. Each day they are to draw or sketch people, buildings, vehicles, designs, or any other interesting things they see. At the end of the week, they are to exchange the notebooks with a partner or share them in small groups.

    ✦ Each participant will need a small mirror for this project. Write a sentence about da Vinci on the chalkboard and tell students to copy it on a sheet of paper. Hold the mirror up to the writing to get an idea of what mirror writing looks like. Challenge students to print the sentence using mirror writing so that when it is held up to a mirror the writing looks normal.

4. Leonardo da Vinci was the proud owner of several cats which he liked to sketch. For homework, assign students the task of making a number of sketches of a pet or other animal. Share the sketches in class the next day. (A good resource for this activity is *Draw 50 Cats* by Lee J. Ames, Doubleday, 1986.)

5. See page 69 of Teacher Created Materials #288, *Explorers,* for additional projects that focus on Leonardo da Vinci.

## Recommended Reading

*The Annotated Mona Lisa* by Carol Strickland, Ph.D., and John Boswell (Andrews and McMeel, 1992)
*Leonardo da Vinci* by Richard McLanathan (Harry N. Abrams, Inc., 1989)
*Leonardo da Vinci* by Ernest Raboff (Harper & Row, 1987)
*The Life and Times of Leonardo da Vinci* by Liana Bortolon (The Curtis Publishing Company, 1967)
*Renaissance Painters Coloring Book* by Andy Nelson (Culpepper Press, 1991)

*Reprinted from TCM 494 Focus on Artists, Teacher Created Materials, Inc., 1994.*

### COMPUTER TECHNOLOGY

1. Read and interpret hardware and software manuals.
2. Comprehend and use symbols, abbreviations, and signs.
3. Use directions for applications, troubleshooting, and networking.
4. Locate specific information on the World Wide Web.
5. Apply reading skills to specific types of literary text.
6. Gather information for research reports.

### FAMILY AND CONSUMER STUDIES

1. Categorize information.
2. Recognize and follow patterns of organization: list, cause/effect, comparison/contrast, and sequence.
3. Evaluate and use information from labels, charts, guarantees, and utility information.
4. Follow directions/evaluate consequences.
5. Evaluate consumer research and advertising.
6. Use and evaluate signs, symbols, and abbreviations.
7. Follow use/care instructions and labels.
8. Evaluate nutritional information.

The following page displays an application of reading in the content area of Family and Consumer Studies.

**Reading in the Content Areas: Family and Consumer Studies**

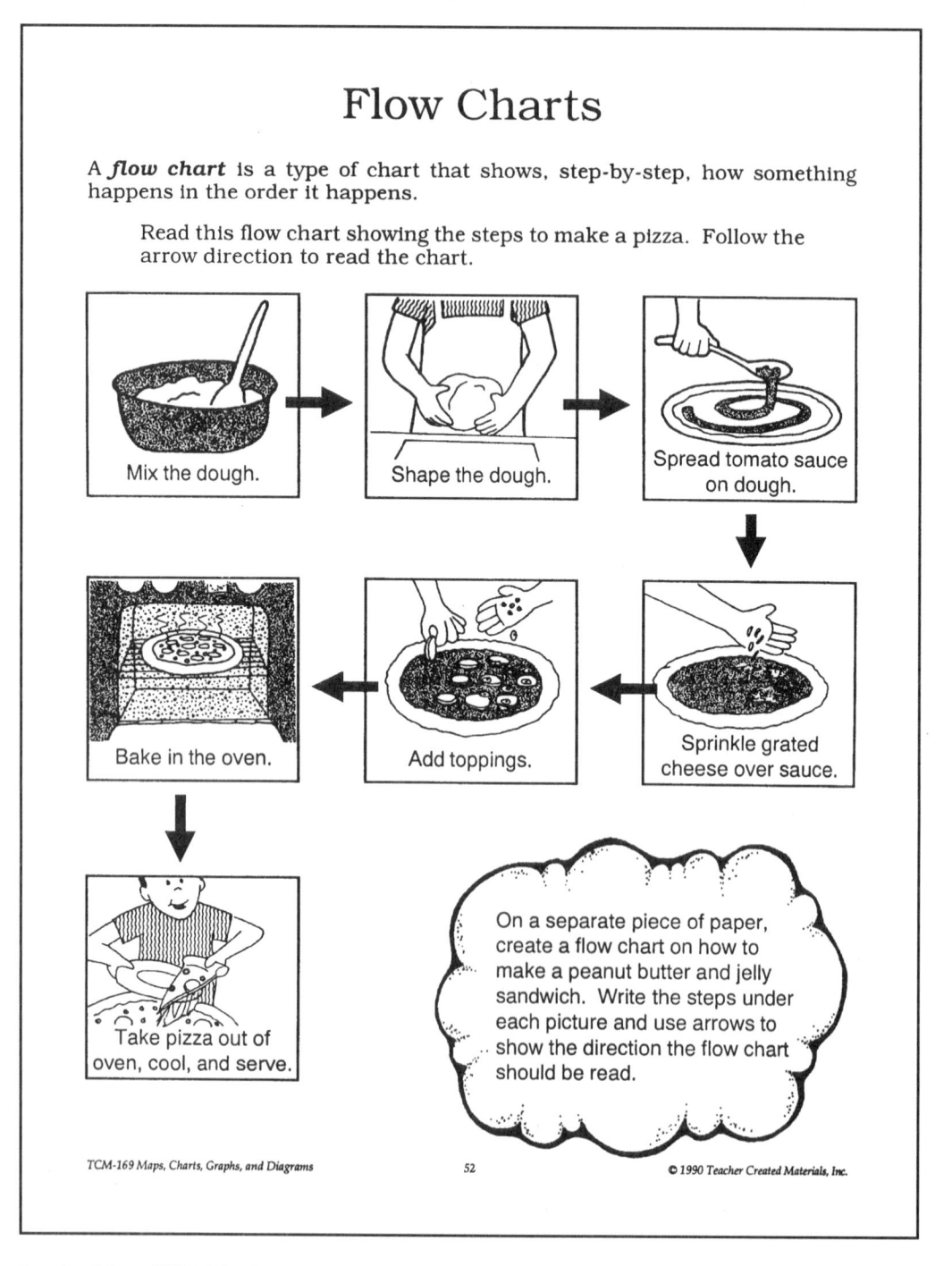

# Flow Charts

A *flow chart* is a type of chart that shows, step-by-step, how something happens in the order it happens.

Read this flow chart showing the steps to make a pizza. Follow the arrow direction to read the chart.

Mix the dough. → Shape the dough. → Spread tomato sauce on dough. ↓
Bake in the oven. ← Add toppings. ← Sprinkle grated cheese over sauce.
↓
Take pizza out of oven, cool, and serve.

On a separate piece of paper, create a flow chart on how to make a peanut butter and jelly sandwich. Write the steps under each picture and use arrows to show the direction the flow chart should be read.

TCM-169 *Maps, Charts, Graphs, and Diagrams*     52     © 1990 Teacher Created Materials, Inc.

*Reprinted from TCM 169 Charts, Graphs, and Diagrams, Teacher Created Materials, Inc., 1994.*

### INDUSTRIAL TECHNOLOGY

1. Use manuals.
2. Evaluate and interpret licenses and guarantees.
3. Evaluate workmanship and quality.
4. Recognize cause and effect.
5. Follow instructions/read blueprints, interpret patterns and layouts.
6. Follow instructions for use of tools and instruments.
7. Learn and follow safety instructions.
8. Use and follow measurements.

### LANGUAGE

1. Apply decoding/phonetic system.
2. Learn new words and link conceptually to English equivalents.
3. Translate and read dialogue.
4. Understand idioms.
5. Make grammatical applications.
6. Read and understand new culture, values, and customs.

### LITERATURE

1. Visualize.
2. Recognize patterns of organization: sequence, cause/effect, and comparison/contrast.
3. Read and understand the classics.
4. Evaluate writing: structure, style, and quality.
5. Experience a story: plot, characters, setting, episodes, style, and language.
6. Read, understand, and interpret various genres.
7. Use words with multiple meanings, figurative language, and connotation and denotation.
8. Read orally/listen to oral readings.
9. Interpret poetry.
10. Recognize tone, purpose, bias, and propaganda.
11. Write in response to reading.

An example of reading in the content area of literature can be viewed on the next page.

# Reading in the Content Areas: Literature

**Culminating Activity**  *Where the Red Fern Grows*

# A Look into the Future

When Billy begins to live in town, he is sure to notice many differences between town life and country life. If you were in his place, how do you think you might compare and contrast them?

Use what you know about the Ozark hills that were Billy's home and his experiences in the town of Tahlequah to complete the comparison chart below. Add your own insights as well!

### Billy's Two Worlds

| Country Life | Town Life |
|---|---|
| **Criterion by which Billy is judged by others** ||
|  |  |
| **Ability to make friends** ||
|  |  |
| **Educational advantages and disadvantages** ||
|  |  |
| **Level of contentment** ||
|  |  |
| **Reasons to stay** ||
|  |  |
| **Reasons to go** ||
|  |  |

In which world would you be happier? Why?

© 1991 Teacher Created Materials, Inc.  #400 Literature Unit

*Reprinted from TCM 400 Where the Red Fern Grows, Teacher Created Materials, Inc., 1991.*

## MATHEMATICS

1. Apply graphic representations to problems and situations.
2. Develop mathematical perspective; weigh evidence of data; evaluate on the basis of principles, cause and effect, and variables.
3. Exercise judgment in distinguishing the important and the irrelevant.
4. Grasp mathematical concepts and relate them to others or generalize from them.
5. Recognize equations as expressive in a manner similar to sentences in prose writing.
6. Use and evaluate mathematical symbols and expressions descriptive of size and shape, extent, and relationships.
7. Read for a specific purpose.
8. Interpret mathematical symbols which are extensions of mathematical terms.
9. Read and solve word problems by using the necessary analytical and computational steps.
10. Analyze and interpret pictorial and graphic representations.
11. Follow directions.

*The reading phase of mathematics utilizes a very precise notation system of words, numbers, and symbols. In most instances, understanding mathematics requires proficiency and fluency in all of them. This is particularly true as mathematics instruction develops beyond the instruction of basic arithmetic principles. Specific instruction for reading mathematics, when given by a reading teacher outside the mathematics classroom, typically consists of artificial workbook activities that result in a minimum of transfer to the mathematics curriculum. Therefore, it is the mathematics teacher in the mathematics classroom who should give the instruction for reading mathematics (Smith and Kepner, 1981, p. 51).*

On the following pages, examples of reading in the content area of mathematics are presented.

## Reading in the Content Areas: Mathematics

*Dealing with Data*            *Mean, Median, Mode, and Range*

# Data Definitions

*Ordering*

It is important to order the data for easy use.

Data is often put in order from smallest to largest.

*Mean*

The mean is the same as the average.

It is found by dividing the sum of the data by the number of pieces of data.

*Median*

The median is the middle piece of data.

If you have 33 items, whatever is in 17th place is the median.

*Mode*

The mode is the most common value in a set of data.

The mode is easy to spot in a graph. You can also find it in an ordered list.

*Range*

The range in a set of data is the difference between the largest and smallest values.

Subtract to find the range.

*Graph*

A graph is a picture of the data in easy-to-understand form.

You can choose among many kinds, such as bar graphs, line graphs, and circle graphs.

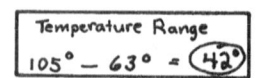

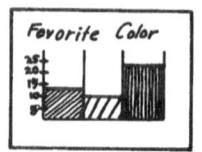

*Reprinted from TCM 658 Activities for Math, Teacher Created Materials, Inc., 1996.*

# Reading in the Content Areas: Mathematics

*Mean, Median, Mode, and Range*  *Dealing with Data*

## Data Capture Sheet

Student _____

Group _____

1. Decide on the features you will need in a used car.

   _____

   _____

   _____

   _____

2. Divide up the newspapers and check the ads. Each person should find at least five ads. Think of some way to keep track of them. (Will you write down page numbers, circle the ads, clip them out?)

   _____

   _____

   _____

3. Put the ads in order by price on another piece of paper.

4. Use a calculator to find the mean price.

   _____

5. Look at your ordered list to find the median price.

   _____

*Reprinted from TCM 658 Activities for Math, Teacher Created Materials, Inc., 1996.*

### MUSIC

1. Read and understand historical and analytical accounts of music, musicians, style, and form.
2. Read and follow lyrics.
3. Use and interpret notes, symbols, abbreviations.
4. Understand foreign terminology.
5. Read and understand historical literature, including biography.

### PHYSICAL EDUCATION and HEALTH

1. Understand scientific writing.
2. Follow a sequence of directions.
3. Interpret and carry out movement skills and safety rules.
4. Interpret data.
5. Use graphs, charts, and tables.
6. Apply written information about health to daily living.
7. Research the history of a sport.
8. Interpret and follow diagrams and signals.
9. Read to understand scoring procedures.

### SCIENCE

1. Comprehend diagrams, charts, tables.
2. Develop scientific thinking by weighing evidence, recognizing patterns of organization such as cause/effect and comparison/contrast, observing and organizing data, drawing conclusions, and categorizing.
3. Read/follow safety instructions and directions.
4. Comprehend and analyze technical style of writing.

Look on the next four pages for examples of reading in the content areas of music, physical education, and science.

# Reading in the Content Areas: Music

The Language of Music_____More About Music

# Musical Terms

The musical terms on this page are part of the language of music. If you learn them, your knowledge can add to an appreciation of the music you hear and play, as well as an appreciation of the composers who have created it. Knowledge of musical terms also can help you understand more about the similarities and differences of music through times, places, and cultures.

*Rhythm* is the recurrence or repetition of beats in a regular, predictable way. It divides the time in musical works, using accented and unaccented beats to create a pattern. Some rhythms make you want to clap and dance while others help you fall asleep. Sample rhythms can be found on page 109.

*Notes* are symbols that show musicians how long to make sounds. Each note stands for a specific time length for a tone to be held. Whole notes are held longer than half-notes, and half-notes are held longer than quarter-notes. More information about notes and their time values can be found on pages 109 and 110.

*Melody* is an organized succession of tones. It is the memorable tune that we sometimes walk about humming or singing!

*Harmony* is the combination of groups of tones sounded together. The basic unit of harmony is the chord, where two or more tones are played together.

*Tone color* is the timbre or special quality of a voice or musical instrument. Tone color distinguishes the tone of one musical instrument or voice from another.

*Form* is the structure of a musical piece. It is the way in which the entire composition is built. Sometimes composers follow certain forms when they create, such as the form of A (statement) — B (contrast) — A (return) in an orchestral work, or the verse and chorus form of many popular songs.

*Pitch* is the highness or lowness of a tone.

*Tempo* is how fast or slow music is played.

*Dynamics* is how loudly or softly the music is played.

*Reprinted from TCM 492 Focus on Composers, Teacher Created Materials, Inc., 1994.*

## Reading in the Content Areas: Music

The Language of Music _____ More About Music

# Simple Note Values and Rhythms

Learning note values and rhythms requires mathematical skill. You must be able to divide and count.

*Notes have specific values.*

| | | |
|---|---|---|
| **one whole note =** | two half notes | 𝅗𝅥 𝅗𝅥 |
| | four quarter notes | ♩ ♩ ♩ ♩ |
| | eight eighth notes | ♪ ♪ ♪ ♪ ♪ ♪ ♪ ♪ |
| **one half note =** | two quarter notes | ♩ ♩ |
| | four eighth notes | ♪ ♪ ♪ ♪ |
| **one quarter note =** | two eighth notes | ♪ ♪ |

**Notes that are dotted add half their value to the note.**

| | | |
|---|---|---|
| **dotted half note =** | three quarter notes | ♩ ♩ ♩ |
| **dotted quarter note =** | three eighth notes | ♪ ♪ ♪ |

*Notes written in musical notation have specific rhythms.* Music is written in measures with a time signature at the beginning of the piece. The top number of the time signature tells you how many beats are in each measure. The bottom number tells you that a note of that value gets one count.

3/4 | ♩ ♩ | ♩ ♩ | ♩ ♩ | ♩. |
    In  our    room  we   love  to   sing.

4/4 | ♩ ♩ ♩ | ♩. ♩ | ♩ ♩ ♩ | ♩ ♩ |
  We  love  to   sing  a   song  all  to-  geth-  er.

Make some songs using the simple note values and rhythms you have learned on this page. The notes provided on page 110 can be cut out and used to create your songs.

©1994 *Teacher Created Materials, Inc.*     #492 *Focus on Composers*

*Reprinted from TCM 492 Focus on Composers, Teacher Created Materials, Inc., 1994.*

# Reading in the Content Areas: Physical Education and Health

*Baseball* _____ *Jackie Robinson*

## Suggested Activities and Extensions

1. Jackie Robinson paved the way for other minority players to enter the major leagues. What do you suppose they would like to say to him if they could meet him today? Write a dialogue between a young rookie of today meeting Robinson and discussing the changes that have taken place in baseball and in America itself.
2. For more information about Jackie Robinson or current players, write to the following address:
    Los Angeles Dodgers
    1000 Elysian Park Avenue
    Los Angeles, California 90012
3. Discuss or write about how you would have felt being Jackie Robinson in 1946. What decision would you have made about "breaking the color line"? Do you think it was his responsibility to do this in order to help other minorities? Explain.
4. Read more about Don Newcombe and Roy Campanella. Summarize the information on trading card forms (page 4).
5. Jackie Robinson played on the major league All-Star team every year from 1949 to 1954. Write a research paper about last year's All-Star game. Where was it held? Who were the players on each team? What were their positions? Who were the managers? What was the final score? What important plays were made?
6. Write to the University of California at Los Angeles (UCLA) for information about Jackie Robinson's athletic accomplishments during his brief stay at that school. Research other black athletes who followed his footsteps at that university.
7. Research the baseball career of Satchel Paige, another black baseball player of extraordinary accomplishment and longevity. Compile a list of his statistics—number of years playing, wins and losses as a pitcher, number of major league starts, etc.
8. Interview someone old enough to have seen Jackie Robinson play baseball. Ask questions about Robinson's abilities on the field, his effect on other players, his effect on the fans, and his effect on the news of the time. Was his influence felt beyond the baseball field? Record your interview on tape if it is all right with the person being interviewed; then play the interview back to the class.

## Related Reading

*All-Time Great World Series* by Andrew Gutelle. Grosset and Dunlap, 1994.
*In the Year of the Boar and Jackie Robinson* by Bette Bao Lord. Harper and Row, 1987.
*Jackie Robinson* by Manfred Weidhorn. Simon & Schuster, 1992.
*Jackie Robinson: Baseball's Civil Rights Legend* by Karen M. Coombs. Enslow Publications, 1997.
*Leagues Apart* by Lawrence S. Ritter. Morrow Junior Books, 1995.
*Shadow Ball* by Geoffrey C. Ward. Knopf, 1994.
*The Story of Negro League Baseball* by William Brashler. Ticknor and Fields, 1994.
*Teammates* by Paul Bacon. Harcourt, Brace, Jovanovich, 1990.
*Take Me Out to the Ball Game* by Jack Norworth. Four Winds Press, 1993 (illustrations of 1947 Ebbets Field).

*Reprinted from TCM 499 Focus on Athletes, Teacher Created Materials, Inc., 1997.*

# Reading in the Content Areas: Science

# Tables

A *table* is a type of chart that is organized in such a way as to make information very easy to find.

Read this table about the three major classifications of rocks. Use the information in the table to answer the questions at the bottom of this page.

### Three Major Classifications of Rocks

| classification | Rock | color | structure |
|---|---|---|---|
| **Igneous Rock** (forms from hardened magma) | granite | white to gray, pink to red | closely arranged medium-to-coarse crystals |
| | obsidian | black, sometimes with brown streaks | glassy, no crystals |
| | pumice | grayish-white | light, fine pores, floats on water |
| **Sedimentary Rock** (formed by hardening of plant, animal, and mineral materials) | coal | shiny to dull black | brittle, in seams or layers |
| | limestone | white, gray, and buff to black and red | dense, forms cliffs and may contain fossils |
| | shale | yellow, red, gray, green, black | dense, fine particles, soft, smells like clay |
| **Metamorphic Rock** (formed by existing rock changing because of heat or pressure) | marble | many colors, often mixed | medium to coarse crystals |
| | quartzite | white, gray, pink, and buff | big, hard, and often glassy |
| | schist | white, gray, red, green, black | flaky, banded, sparkles with mica |

1. What is the name of the igneous rock that is black and has a glassy appearance? _____

2. What classification of rock is most likely to contain fossils?
   _____

3. To which classification do schist and marble belong?
   _____

* Find other examples of tables and share them with your class.

© 1990 Teacher Created Materials, Inc.   TCM-169 Maps, Charts, Graphs, and Diagrams

*Reprinted from TCM 169 Charts, Graphs, and Diagrams, Teacher Created Materials, Inc., 1994.*

## SOCIAL SCIENCES

1. Comprehend and evaluate facts, ideas, principles and practices.
2. Establish appropriate relationships of events in chronological order; recognize sequence pattern of organization.
3. Evaluate controversial issues.
4. Follow graphic presentations such as line, statistical, trend, functional, bar, and circle graphs.
5. Interpret social, geographical, historical, political, and legal terms.
6. Investigate and test the reliability of statements or authors and agreements or differences among authorities.
7. Visualize and interpret other times, places, and circumstances.
8. Realize the relevance of the subject matter.
9. Locate information/research.

The following page provides an example of reading in the content area of social studies.

# Reading in the Content Areas: Social Sciences

*The Vietnam War*

# Vietnam Stats

Until the Tet Offensive in 1968, the majority of the American people had supported the war in Vietnam. The staggering statistics about the wounded and dead, however, shocked everyone. It was one of the reasons that so many people began calling for an end to the war. Examine the statistics in the box below and answer the questions that follow.

| Year | American Troops in Vietnam | American Deaths in Vietnam |
|------|----------------------------|----------------------------|
| 1965 | 180,000 | 1,728 |
| 1966 | 380,000 | 6,053 |
| 1967 | 450,000 | 11,058 |
| 1968 | 540,000 | 17,622 |
| 1969 | 543,000 | 11,527 |
| 1970 | 280,000 | 6,065 |
| 1971 | 140,000 | 2,348 |
| 1972 | 70,000 | 561 |

1. In which year were the most American troops in Vietnam? _____
2. In which year were the fewest American troops in Vietnam? _____
3. What is the difference between the figures from question one and question two above? _____
4. In which year did the casualty figures peak? _____
5. In which years was the death toll more than 11,000? _____  _____  _____
6. What is the difference between the number of deaths in 1965 and the number of deaths in 1972? _____
7. What is the total number of American deaths in Vietnam for 1965 to 1969? _____
8. What is the number of American troops who served in Vietnam from 1965 to 1972? _____
9. Of the troops in Vietnam in 1966, approximately what percentage died? _____
10. Of the troops in Vietnam in 1968, approximately what percentage died? _____

*Reprinted from TCM 2028 The Sixties, Challenging, Teacher Created Materials, Inc., 1998.*

# Readability

Readability formulas were introduced more than thirty years ago in an effort to give teachers and administrators a tool to use in choosing textbooks suitable to the grade level of intended use. Certainly, these formulas have limitations, but they also offer a starting point for choosing reading materials appropriate for students. There are many formulas available, but the Fry Readability Graph has proven accurate and reliable over many years of use for estimates of textbook difficulty. It uses sentence length and word length to identify the grade-level difficulty of reading material. The graph and directions for use can be found on the next page.

Assumptions and limitations of readability are many. A readability formula does not take into consideration:

- student background experience or conceptual framework
- multiple word meanings, specialized word meanings, subtle connotations, or figurative language
- abstract concepts
- student interest/motivation

A readability formula offers a starting point—an estimate of text difficulty. The information it provides should be coupled with teacher judgment of text characteristics and student factors. The readability work sheet on page 49 combines the information from the Fry test with subjective information that the teacher provides after careful consideration. This process should prove quite useful in finding appropriate material for every student. Remember, though, a textbook or piece of text should not be discarded or dropped from consideration based solely on readability. Once the instructional level of the material is known, directed reading strategies can be utilized to facilitate access and meaning making. An example of the Fry Readability Graph is found on page 48 followed by a sample work sheet.

> **Once the instructional level of the material is known, directed reading strategies can be utilized to facilitate access and meaning making.**

**Fry Readability Graph**

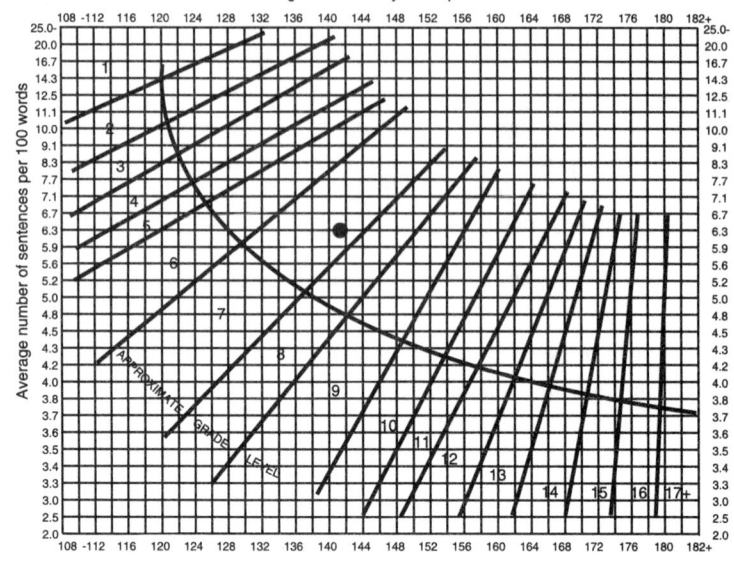

Average number of syllables per 100 words

1. Randomly select three (3) sample passages and count out exactly 100 words each, beginning with the beginning of a sentence. Do count proper nouns, initializations, and numerals.
2. Count the number of sentences in the 100 words, estimating the length of the fraction of the last sentence to the nearest one-tenth.
3. Count the total number of syllables in the 100-word passage. If you don't have a hand counter available, an easy way is simply to put a mark above every syllable over one in each word, then when you get to the end of a passage, count the number of marks and add 100. Small calculators can also be used as counters by pushing the numeral 1 and then pushing the + sign for each word or syllable.
4. Enter the graph with the average sentence length and average number of syllables; plot the dot where the two lines intersect. The area where the dot is plotted will give you the approximate grade level.
5. If a great deal of variability is found in syllable count or sentence count, putting more samples into the average is desirable.
6. A word is defined as a group of symbols with a space on either side; thus, 1945 is one word.
7. A syllable is defined as a phonetic syllable. Generally, there are as many syllables as vowel sounds. For example, *stopped* is one syllable and *wanted* is two syllables. When counting syllables for numbers and initializations, count one syllable for each symbol. For example, 1945 is four syllables.

*Source: Edward Fry, Rutgers University Reading Center, New Brunswick, NJ 08904 (Reproduction Permitted)*

# Readability

Title of Book: _____

Publishers: _____ Recommended Level: _____

Date of Publication: _____ Author: _____

Student Friendly?    Yes    Somewhat    No

Curriculum/Content:    Excellent    Good    Fair    Poor    Mixed

Issues of Equity: _____ Diverse representation throughout text
                  _____ Some diversity
                  _____ No aspects of multiculturation

**Passage 1**

     page      from      to      # of sentences    # of syllables

    _____ _____ _____ _____ _____

**Passage 2**

     page      from      to      # of sentences    # of syllables

    _____ _____ _____ _____ _____

**Passage 3**

     page      from      to      # of sentences    # of syllables

    _____ _____ _____ _____ _____

                          Total: _____ _____

                         Average: _____ _____

                    Fry Readability = _____

Comments: _____
_____
_____
_____
_____
_____

## Concluding Remarks

By promoting content reading strategies, teachers add tools to their repertoire that shift the educational focus from teaching to learning, from passive acquisition of facts and routines to the active application of ideas to problems. Placing students in collaborative problem-solving groups and providing reading assignments that require analysis and creativity can develop higher order cognitive skills.

Content literacy strategies help the underprepared student as well as the gifted. They are vital for remedial students and those who speak English as a second language because they offer opportunities to clarify concepts and receive help with technical and specialized vocabulary. In addition, students with higher literacy skills are provided a chance to teach, commonly acknowledged as the best way to learn a subject!

Most important, remember the following principles of effective instruction; these will facilitate the integration of reading into content teaching:

- Be sure that text material is suited in difficulty to the reading levels of the students; if text material is difficult, incorporate directed reading strategies to help students access, comprehend, and interpret print.
- Encourage students to read widely in related content materials.
- Give adequate time to introducing the book, showing textbook parts, modeling note-taking and outlining.
- Give adequate instruction/attention to technical and specialized vocabulary.
- Teach concepts and vocabulary that are important for understanding each unit.
- Use formative and summative methods of authentic assessment.
- Teach the specialized reading skills that students need in order to understand a subject matter.
- Give clear/concise directions for assignments. Directions should be given orally and in writing.
- Teach students to use appropriate reference materials.
- Provide adequate reference and supplemental reading materials.
- Provide a wide range of materials at various reading levels to accommodate and encourage students at many achievement levels.
- Encourage students to read for pleasure as well as information.
- Help poor readers develop adequate reading skills. Also help

**By promoting content reading strategies, teachers add tools to their repertoire that shift the educational focus from teaching to learning, from passive acquisition of facts and routines to the active application of ideas to problems.**

them locate school and community resources for literacy tutoring.
- Know the reading levels of materials that students will use.
- Know the attitudes and interests of students.
- Assess the reading abilities of students.
- Assess student ability to use the study skills necessary for each subject area.
- Provide high interest/motivational reading materials.
- MOST IMPORTANT: Be a role model for students—let them know and see that the teacher likes to read.

> **Be a role model for students—let them know and see that the teacher likes to read.**

# Expanding Vocabulary and Conceptual Framework

**Students need a wide range of experiences to develop and expand their conceptual frameworks, and they need an ever-growing vocabulary in order to comprehend increasingly complex subject area material.**

Words label the concepts that are formed as a result of experiences. Students need a wide range of experiences to develop and expand their conceptual frameworks, and they need an ever-growing vocabulary in order to comprehend increasingly complex subject area material. Throughout middle and secondary school years, vocabulary development should help students

- become adept at using a variety of word recognition strategies.
- systematically increase sight vocabulary.
- unlock meanings of technical and specialized words in each content area.
- establish a systematic, lifelong method of vocabulary inquiry.
- become motivated and enthusiastic about WORDS!

## Word Recognition Skills

Ask students how they "attack" an unfamiliar word they meet in a reading assignment. Most will say, "I skip it." It is easier to avoid the word than to stop and consider the meaning. Many students don't have a clue about how to unlock the meaning of a new word. Many don't realize that an unfamiliar word in print might be familiar to them in their listening or speaking vocabularies.

All teachers should incorporate word recognition strategies in every lesson; to do so, teachers must have a firm grasp of the principles of word recognition. Use the following "test" to check your own base of word recognition knowledge:

## WORD RECOGNITION SKILLS CHECK FOR TEACHERS

Directions: Mark true or false for each question.

_____ 1. Different types of word recognition skills are separate and distinct and can easily be divided and taught by grade level.

_____ 2. If the elementary reading program is successful, a middle grade teacher can assume that students have the word recognition skills necessary for reading at the secondary level.

_____ 3. A competent reader normally uses just one technique of attacking an unfamiliar word.

_____ 4. Vowel letters in open syllables usually have a long sound.

_____ 5. Mastery of letter sounds is most likely to occur if the letter sounds are taught in isolation.

_____ 6. A consonant digraph consists of two letters blended together so that sounds of each of the consonants are heard when the word is pronounced.

_____ 7. An open syllable ends in a consonant.

_____ 8. The most useful word recognition tool is phonics.

_____ 9. Research is clear that the best way to teach reading is by intensive phonics instruction.

_____ 10. Words that have a similar appearance (*cow* and *now, boil* and *bowl*) are good examples of words that can be recognized by using configuration clues.

_____ 11. The words *or, owl,* and *bird* contain good examples of the schwa sound.

_____ 12. A diphthong is a combination of two vowels that make a sound unlike that of either vowel in isolation.

_____ 13. A syllable must contain a vowel or vowel sound.

_____ 14. Vowel sounds are easier to teach than consonant sounds.

_____ 15. Some letters of the alphabet have no sounds of their own.

_____ 16. Teaching word-recognition skills belongs primarily in grades one through three.

_____ 17. The use of structural analysis can help a student identify an unknown word by its prefix or suffix.

_____ 18. Using an eclectic approach to teach word recognition skills gives students the best chance of becoming competent in their ability to identify unfamiliar words.

_____ 19. The "a" in *car* has a short vowel sound.

_____ 20. The "e" in *set* has a long sound.

_____ 21. A digraph represents one sound that has been formed by a combination of letters.

_____ 22. The "ow" in *howl* is a diphthong.

_____ 23. Word recognition skills are best taught when integrated with other types of reading instruction rather than isolated.

_____ 24. The "y" in *by* is a consonant.

_____ 25. The "o" in *button* is represented by the schwa sound.

_____ 26. If a syllable is closed, its vowel sound is usually short.

_____ 27. The sound of a vowel that is followed by the letter r, l, or w is often controlled by the r, l, or w.

> **All teachers should incorporate word recognition strategies in every lesson; to do so, teachers must have a firm grasp of the principles of word recognition.**

_____ 28. In attempting to unlock a new word, the child should first sound out all letters.

_____ 29. Context clues are usually the fastest way to unlock the meaning of an unfamiliar word.

_____ 30. In a single syllable word ending with "e", the "e" is usually silent and the preceding vowel is short.

_____ 31. When the letter "e" falls at the end of a one-syllable word, it is usually silent.

_____ 32. If a student can not recognize the difference between similar letters or words (*b/d, bad/dad*), visual discrimination may need further testing.

_____ 33. Inability to recognize words such as *here, the, he,* or *it,* indicates that the student is not using context clues.

_____ 34. If a student meets an unfamiliar word in print, the best advice is "use the dictionary!"

_____ 35. *Mississippi* and *monkey* are easily recognized through the use of configuration clues.

**It is impossible to demonstrate how to use a pronunciation key, look for roots and prefixes, or sound out a difficult word without having a strong foundation in the principles of word recognition.**

The answers:

| | | | | | | |
|---|---|---|---|---|---|---|
| 1. F | 6. F | 11. F | 16. F | 21. T | 26. T | 31. T |
| 2. F | 7. F | 12. T | 17. T | 22. T | 27. T | 32. T |
| 3. F | 8. F | 13. T | 18. T | 23. T | 28. F | 33. F |
| 4. T | 9. F | 14. F | 19. F | 24. T | 29. T | 34. F |
| 5. F | 10. F | 15. T | 20. F | 25. T | 30. F | 35. T |

If teacher knowledge of word recognition skills is limited, many "teaching moments" will be lost. It is impossible to demonstrate how to use a pronunciation key, look for roots and prefixes, or sound out a difficult word without having a strong foundation in the principles of word recognition. For help in this area, the following sources are excellent:

* Bishop, Ashley, and Suzanne Bishop. *Professional's Guide: Teaching Phonics, Phonemic Awareness, and Word Recognition.* Westminster: Teacher Created Materials, Inc., 1997.

* Cunningham, Patricia M. *Phonics They Use: Words for Reading and Writing.* 2nd Ed. New York: HarperCollins, 1995.

* Fry, Edward. *How to Teach Reading: For Teachers, Parents, Tutors.* Westminster: Teacher Created Materials, Inc. 1995.

* Fry, Edward Bernard, Dona Lee Fountoukidis, and Jacqueline Kress Polk. *The Reading Teacher's Book of Lists,* 3rd Ed. Englewood Cliffs: Prentice-Hall, Inc., 1998.

* Harris, Theodore L., and Richard E. Hodges, Editors. *The Literacy Dictionary: The Vocabulary of Reading and Writing.* Newark: International Reading Association, 1995.

* Heilman, Arthur W. *Phonics in Proper Perspective,* 8th Ed. Merrill Publishing Company, 1997.

* Strickland, Dorothy S. *Teaching Phonics Today: A Primer for Educators.* Newark: International Reading Association, 1998.

Students should routinely practice and utilize the following word recognition skills:
- context clues
- phonetic analysis
- structural analysis
- using a dictionary
- configuration clues
- text aids

Teachers should never assume that students know these skills or how to utilize them. Rather, students must be taught how to use the strategies, have plenty of guided practice, and routinely view the teacher modeling these techniques.

Ruddell (1997) offers a system for revealing the meaning of unfamiliar words called CSSR (Context, Structure, Sound, Reference). First, students use context clues: punctuation, examples, synonyms, and antonyms. Second, they look for familiar structure in the word—a root, prefix, or suffix that might have meaning. Then, students try sounding out the word to see if it sounds familiar. Finally, they rely on reference sources: dictionary, CD-ROM, thesaurus, and encyclopedia. CSSR provides students with a systematic way of independently developing vocabulary.

## Increasing Sight Vocabulary

Wide reading experience is probably the best way of continually enlarging a child's stock of sight words, but planned instructional activities are also quite beneficial. These include the following:

- flashcards
- labeling
- language experience
- synonyms and antonyms
- multiple meanings
- newspaper scavenger hunts
- categorizing (accompanying storytelling or oral discussion)
- oral discussion + semantic mapping
- building experiential background
- concept cards
- Cloze
- picture cues
- word art
- word banks

**Wide reading experience is probably the best way of continually enlarging a child's stock of sight words, but planned instructional activities are also quite beneficial.**

## Technical and Specialized Words

"Vocabulary is as unique to a content area as fingerprints are to a human being. A content area is distinguishable by its language, particularly the special and technical vocabulary terms that provide labels for the concepts undergirding the subject matter" (Vacca, 1996, p. 132). A student's store of word knowledge consists of the following:

- General Vocabulary: common, everyday kinds of words
- Specialized Vocabulary: words that take on new, special meanings as they are used in various content areas
- Technical Vocabulary: words that only belong to a particular subject area

Technical and specialized meanings, figurative language, and subtle connotations of words are particularly troublesome for students, especially those who speak English as a second language. For example, a student must count the beats in music, beat an egg in home economics, and try to beat the other team in PE. Teachers must take special care in ensuring that students grasp contextual meaning. By using pre-reading, during reading, and post reading strategies, acquisition of subject matter vocabulary can be facilitated.

## Vocabulary and Conceptual Development Strategies
### Pre-Reading/During Reading/Post Reading

- ◆ Categorization
- ◆ Word Parts
- ◆ Word Origins
- ◆ Context Clues
- ◆ Punctuation
    - Examples
    - Synonyms
- ◆ Vocabulary Inquiry/Self-Study Collection
- ◆ Word Bank
- ◆ Word Map/Semantic Map/Graphic Organizer/Concept Map
- ◆ Writing Activities
- ◆ Puzzles and Word Games

On the next few pages, find information about each of these vocabulary development strategies as well as samples of content related vocabulary activities for creating student motivation and interest in vocabulary building.

## Categorization

Students extend vocabulary through categorization exercises by determining relationships of terms. Examine this example of a word sort from a unit on nutrition. The teacher asked the class to classify the following list of terms under the broad headings of Vitamins, Minerals, Carbohydrates, and Proteins:

| | | | |
|---|---|---|---|
| calcium | animal | immunity | inorganic |
| niacin | A, D, E | starch | sugar |
| riboflavin | vegetable | fat-soluble | zinc |
| ascorbic acid | cellulose | amino acids | energy |

## Word Parts

Morphemic analysis is a valuable text meaning strategy that helps students manage longer words. Look at the following word; although it isn't the longest word in the English language, the students certainly think it is as they watch it fill the chalkboard!

PNEUMONOULTRAMICROSCOPICSILICOVOLCANOCONIOSIS

Ask students to pick out recognizable pieces of the word.

Then, draw the meanings from them:

**pneumono** What illness does it look like? If you have this illness, what is wrong?

**ultra** Yes, it's the name of a detergent; why is it called "Ultra?"

**micro** What other word has micro in it? Microscope! What is a microscope used for?

**scopic** No, it's not a mouthwash! What other words does it look like? What does it mean?

**silico** What does it remind you of? What is silicon?

**volcano** What does a volcano do?

**coni** Besides lava and rock, what covers the earth for miles around the site of a volcano eruption?

**osis** What does it mean to have halitosis? Can you think of other conditions that end in osis?

Finally, put it all together. What is this condition? How might someone get this illness?

Another strategy for teaching meanings of prefixes, suffixes, and root words is to have students work in corroborative groups to create creatures using various word parts. First, they create a name for their creature using eight word parts, and then they draw it using markers, crayons, and butcher paper. Their classmates try to guess the name of the creature. By the end of a lesson, students will know the meanings of thirty or more word parts—and they are not likely to forget them!

Word parts are most effectively taught in the context of a lesson, not as a skill and drill exercise in memorization.

> Morphemic analysis is a valuable text meaning strategy that helps students manage longer words.

## Word Origins

The etymology of a word may be fascinating. Pointing out a few examples to students will create interest and motivate them to independently study words. There are countless books on the origins of the English language, but a few favorites follow:

Almond, Jordan. *Dictionary of Word Origins: A History of the Words, Expressions, and Cliches We Use.* New York: Citadel Press, 1995.

Martin Manser. *Guinness Book of Words.* (out of print but available in many libraries).

Lederer, Richard. *Crazy English.* New York: Simon and Schuster, Inc., 1989.

## Context Clues

Students need to be taught how to look for clues in the sentence in which an unfamiliar word appears (the context of the unfamiliar word). Such clues might include synonyms, antonyms, or examples, and many times an author will use signal words or special punctuation to help the reader locate meaning. Look at these examples:

***Synonym Context Clue:*** *Coalition*

Individual political organizations sometimes unite to form coalitions—partnerships—to increase the support for their ideas.

(Notice the punctuation clue: the synonym is set apart by dashes. Commas are often used, also.)

***Antonym Context Clue:*** *Fallible*

Children often believe their parents are *perfect;* however, when they become teenagers, parents suddenly become quite *fallible.*

(Notice how this clue uses the signal word "however." Other signals for antonyms include *yet, but,* and *although.*)

***Example Context Clue:*** *Innovation*

William Henry Harrison's 1840 campaign brought many innovations to the art of electioneering. *For instance, never before had a presidential candidate been allowed to campaign on his own behalf.* (This example clue is signaled by "for instance." Other example clues are *for example, including, such as,* and *to illustrate.*)

## Vocabulary Inquiry/Self-Study Collection

The conceptual basis for the following vocabulary inquiry strategy finds its roots in the Vocabulary Self-Collection Strategy (VSS) developed by Ruddell. She describes VSS as an "instructional strategy intended to foster long-term acquisition and development of the vocabulary of academic disciplines" (1997, p. 111). The steps in

> **Students need to be taught how to look for clues in the sentence in which an unfamiliar word appears (the context of the unfamiliar word).**

Vocabulary Inquiry are somewhat different from those in Ruddell's VSS, evolving from trial and adaptations of the original strategy. I use Vocabulary Inquiry routinely with my developmental reading students and find that they (1) love it and (2) internalize word meanings because of it!

## Vocabulary Inquiry

*Supplies needed:*

> Butcher paper, markers, at least one dictionary for each group, index cards

*Directions:*

1. Students read a selection (chapter, story, etc.).
2. Students work in cooperative groups of 3–4 students.
3. From the reading selection, each group finds one word that they will nominate for vocabulary study to the entire class. As they look for the word, they should use their word banks (see page 60) to record several choices for consideration.
4. On a sheet of butcher paper, students write the word, its phonetic pronunciation, part of speech, a synonym, and the original sentence where the word appeared.
5. Word sheets are taped to the board, and each group teaches its word to the class. As words are being taught, all students make an index card for self-study. Be prepared—this student teaching is apt to generate a lot of class discussion!
6. As homework, each student writes an original sentence correctly using the word in context.

**Be prepared—this student teaching is apt to generate a lot of class discussion!**

The following is a sample Vocabulary Self-Study card:

---
**asylum**

(ə-sīʹləm)

***Synonyms:*** sanctuary, place of peace or refuge
***Part of Speech:*** noun

---

*(Front of Card)*

---
***Context:*** In this great American *asylum*, the poor of Europe have by some means met together.

***Student's Original Sentence:*** Immigrants found that America was an asylum, a place of refuge.

---

*(Back of Card)*

Each student should have a large (3-inch) notebook ring to keep cards intact. The teacher should routinely read original sentences, use them as examples for class discussion, and have students share with the class in order to reinforce the value of vocabulary study and to praise student efforts.

## WORD BANK

**Directions:** Place this in your binder and use it to keep a record of any word you see or hear that sounds interesting to you. Find a synonym for each word you list. Then, connect each word to something you already know. An example is done for you.

| Word | Synonym(s) | Connection! |
|---|---|---|
| Example: voracious | greedy hungry | Uncle Frank's appetite at Thanksgiving |
|  |  |  |
|  |  |  |
|  |  |  |
|  |  |  |
|  |  |  |
|  |  |  |
|  |  |  |
|  |  |  |
|  |  |  |
|  |  |  |
|  |  |  |
|  |  |  |
|  |  |  |
|  |  |  |
|  |  |  |
|  |  |  |

## Word Map/Semantic Map

Word maps and graphic organizers are visual representations of words, concepts, and their relationships. They help students clarify and enrich their store of word meanings. The following are examples of a concept/word web and a prefix circle.

## Word Web

What does courage mean to you? Use the word web below to brainstorm all the ideas that come to your mind when you think of the word courage.

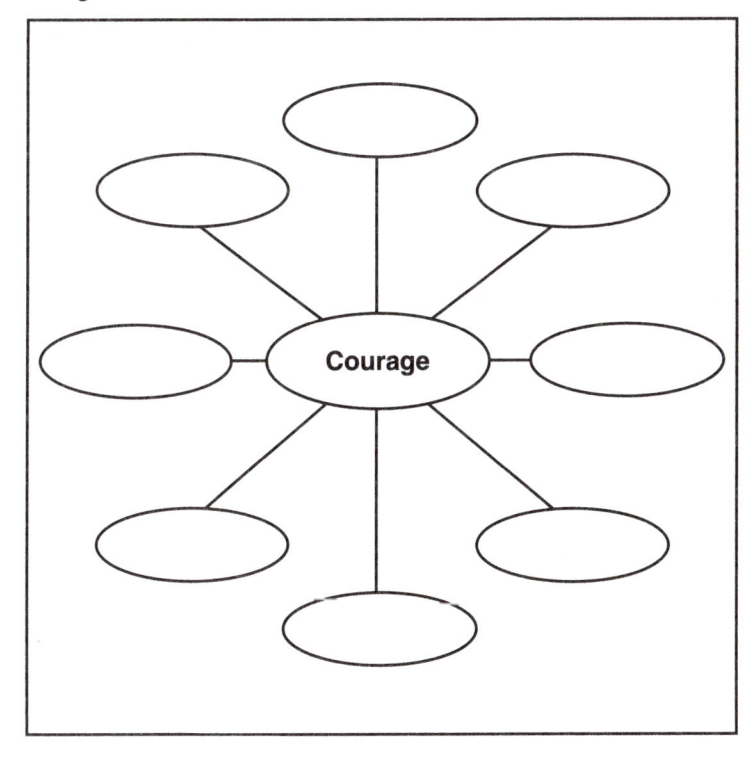

> **Word maps and graphic organizers are visual representations of words, concepts, and their relationships.**

*Reprinted from TCM 472, Learning Through Literature—U.S. History, Teacher Created Materials, Inc., 1994.*

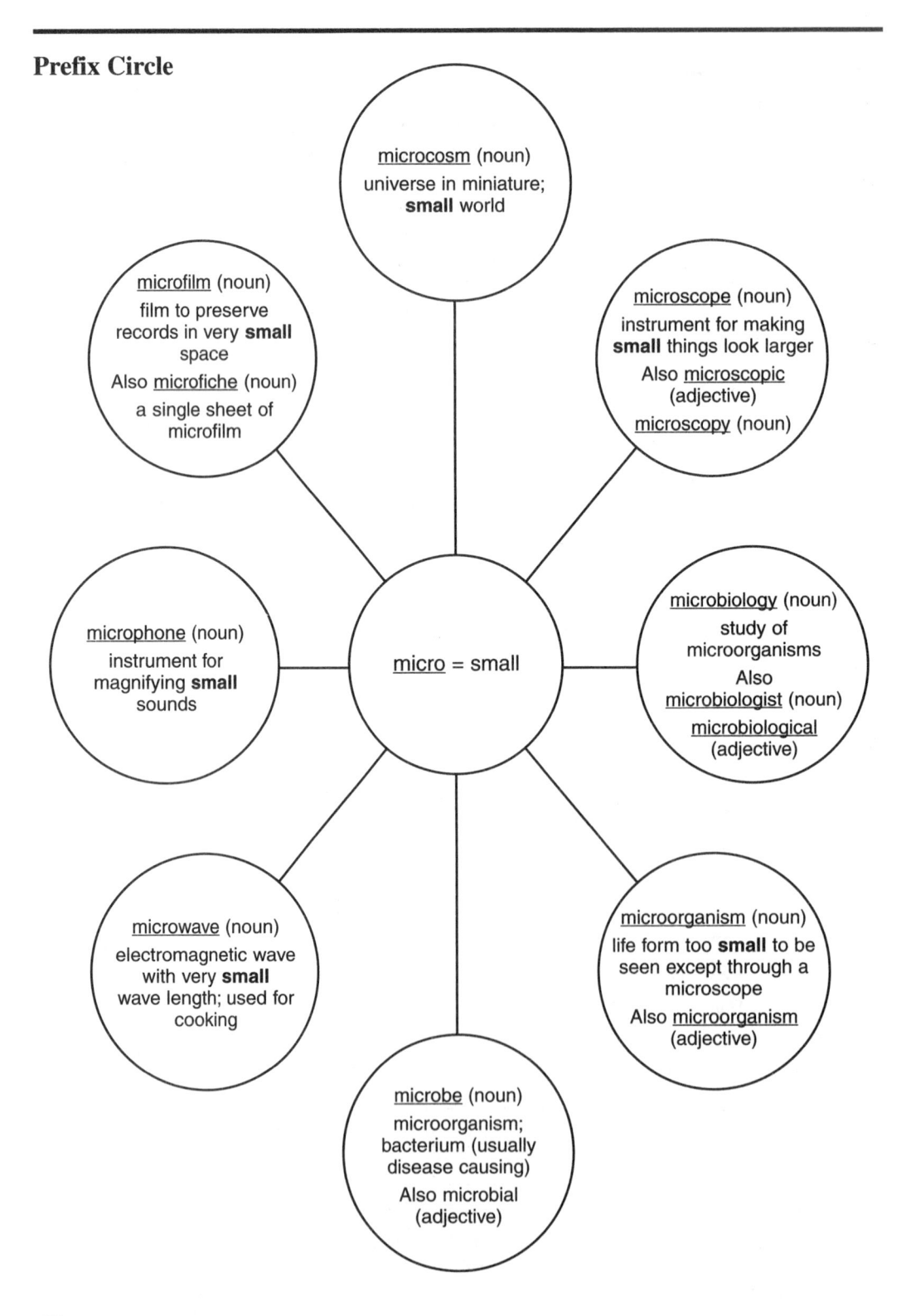

**Prefix Circle**

**micro = small**

- **microcosm** (noun)
  universe in miniature; **small** world

- **microfilm** (noun)
  film to preserve records in very **small** space
  Also microfiche (noun) a single sheet of microfilm

- **microscope** (noun)
  instrument for making **small** things look larger
  Also microscopic (adjective)
  microscopy (noun)

- **microphone** (noun)
  instrument for magnifying **small** sounds

- **microbiology** (noun)
  study of microorganisms
  Also microbiologist (noun)
  microbiological (adjective)

- **microwave** (noun)
  electromagnetic wave with very **small** wave length; used for cooking

- **microorganism** (noun)
  life form too **small** to be seen except through a microscope
  Also microorganism (adjective)

- **microbe** (noun)
  microorganism; bacterium (usually disease causing)
  Also microbial (adjective)

## Writing Activities

In *Integrating Literature in Content Areas,* Carl Walley (1995) and Kate Walley (1995) state that an effective method of teaching students key vocabulary words is to have them develop a log of terminology associated with a content area subject. This can help students understand that each content area has specific interpretations of certain words. In the log, they record the word, a written definition, and, most important, a simple picture illustrating the word. This may be easy or difficult, depending on the complexity of the word or concept. Through writing and drawing, students can more easily attach a word to their conceptual frameworks.

## Puzzles and Word Games

Resources and ideas for vocabulary puzzles and games are endless, but there are a few important points to consider when including games and puzzles in instruction:

- They should be directly related to the topic of study.
- They should alternate between friendly, team competition and those that are played individually.
- They should not be overused.
- They should utilize word meanings and critical thinking skills.

The next few pages provide examples of vocabulary games that can be adapted to any content area.

BINGO can be played in any content area. The teacher can make the bingo cards, or the students can fill in their own from a list placed on the board or overhead. Below is a sample card for "Literary Bingo!"

| allegory | character | genre | Theme | Personifi-cation |
|---|---|---|---|---|
| tone | point of view | fable | Setting | denotation |
| metaphor | epiphany | BINGO | fiction | biography |
| alliteration | symbol | plot | protagonist | connotation |
| fable | narrator | allusion | simile | fore-shadowing |

Directions: Be sure students have markers. Read each definition. If a student recognizes a matching term, a marker is placed accordingly. The first one to correctly match five in a row wins IF that person can give the term and the correct definition.

> Through writing and drawing, students can more easily attach a word to their conceptual frameworks.

## Vocab-pardy

| Antonym | Synonym | Word Part Used Correctly? |
|---|---|---|
| 100 | 100 | 100 |
| 200 | 200 | 200 |
| 300 | 300 | 300 |
| 400 | 400 | 400 |
| 500 | 500 | 500 |

**Directions:** Divide the class into 4 teams. The team decides which category and amount of money to try for. Once the clue is read, whichever team raises hands first gets to try for the answer; they have 10 seconds. If they don't get it right, they lose that number of points, and other teams can raise hands.

## Definitionary

This game is a classroom adaptation of *Pictionary*. Students will draw symbols, pictures, or give definitions on paper to their partners to reinforce or teach the meaning of content vocabulary.

**Directions**

1. Divide the students into groups of three.
2. Give each group one paper tablet and a pencil.
3. Establish categories for the definitions; write them on the board.
   *Example:* composition terms = blue card; poetic terms = purple card
4. Establish dice rules.
   *Example:* a roll of 1 or 3 = blue card, 2 or 4 = purple card, 3 or 6 = gray card

**Playing the Game**

1. The teacher rolls the dice to determine which category will be used.
2. The teacher then picks the card from the appropriate pile and shows the word to the person in each group who will be the first to draw.
3. If the word is a specialized vocabulary word, the teacher will read a short definition to accompany the word.
4. The first group to guess the word from the student's drawing or symbols is the winner of that round.
5. The winners of each round are rewarded.
6. The game can be played for a certain number of rounds or until the teacher runs out of words.

*Note:* The hardest part of this game is preparing the word cards. You must decide which words will be accompanied by no definition, a small definition, or a detailed definition.

## Geometry Concentration

**MATERIALS:** Set of 20 geometry Concentration cards. (Ten cards have geometric terms, and ten have geometric figures.)

Geometry Concentration is played like the traditional game of *Concentration*. To begin, cards should be shuffled and placed facedown in five rows of four cards each. Player one is allowed to turn over two cards. If they form a pair by naming and illustrating a geometry term, the player gets to keep that pair and turn over another two cards. If the cards do not match, the next player takes a turn.

The game is over when all cards have been paired or when no more pairs can be made. The winner is the player with the most matching cards.

# Geometry Concentration Cards

| | | | | |
|---|---|---|---|---|
| Lines l and m | <4 and <6 | TRANSVERSE | COMPLEMENTARY ANGLES | CORRESPONDING ANGLES |
| <1 and <2 | <1 and <2 | PARALLEL LINES | PERPENDICULAR LINES | ALTERNATE EXTERIOR ANGLES |
| <3 and <7 | Line t | <1 and <2 | ADJACENT LINES | SUPPLEMENTARY ANGLES |
| Lines l and m | <2 and <8 | <1 and <3 | VERTICAL LINES | ALTERNATE INTERIOR ANGLES |

65

*America at War—Civil War*

# Battle of Gettysburg Crossword Puzzle

Based on the facts of the battle of Gettysburg you learned from the book, complete the crossword puzzle below.

**Across**
1. Nickname of Thomas J. Jackson
2. Civil War's bloodiest battle
7. Region against slavery
10. Army that retreated
11. Region for slavery

**Down**
1. First state to withdraw from the Union
3. Gray-headed Commander of Confederate troops
4. Maine Commander Colonel Joshua _____
5. Area of giant boulders, jumbled masses of rock and crevices
6. Presidential candidate against slavery
8. Constantly wrote love letters to fiancée
9. Became Commanding General of Union army in June 1863

*Reprinted from TCM 472, Learning Through Literature—U.S. History, Teacher Created Materials, Inc., 1994.*

## Concluding Remarks

Teachers must motivate students and create interest in WORDS! Classrooms should be word-rich environments, places where students see, hear, read, write, and use words, words, and more words! Too often, vocabulary study is tedious and simply an exercise in rote memorization. "Probably the most frequently used inappropriate technique is that of giving students a list of words out of context and telling them to look up their meanings in the dictionary" (Ryder and Graves, 1998, p. 48). Rather, create a word-rich environment for students with daily opportunities for them to inquire, extend, and reinforce word knowledge and conceptual schemata. Word sorts, categorization, concept circles, analogies, graphic organizers, semantic mapping, Cloze, word puzzles, and word games are just a few of the interactive vocabulary strategies that can be utilized to increase student word knowledge. Vocabulary development must be an active part of the curriculum across all disciplines. Students are motivated by teacher enthusiasm, and in turn they are inspired to value words as the basis for language and learning.

**Classrooms should be word-rich environments, places where students see, hear, read, write, and use words, words, and more words!**

# Using Content Literacy Strategies to Improve Comprehension

> **This meaning that a reader makes is a product of the interaction of existing knowledge with information in the text.**

### Reading Comprehension: An Overview

Comprehension is an active process where the reader constructs meaning from print. This meaning that a reader makes is a product of the interaction of existing knowledge with information in the text. "The meaning of words cannot be 'added up' to give the meaning of the whole. The click of comprehension occurs only when the reader evolves a schema that explains the whole message" (Anderson, 1993, p.39). Harold Herber (1978) hypothesizes that comprehension occurs at various levels: literal, inferential and applied. "In literal comprehension, readers identify information that authors present. In interpretive comprehension readers conceptualize ideas that authors imply. In applied comprehension readers synthesize generalization out of a connection between their own ideas and the authors" (Herber & Herber, 1993, p. 215).

*Literal Comprehension:* This is reading the lines (Gray, 1960). The answer is textually explicit (Pearson & Johnson, 1978) and can be found on the page. Literal comprehension does not require interpretation. Details are usually literal—how many, what color, a place, a date.

*Inferential Comprehension:* This is reading between the lines (Gray, 1960). Inferential comprehension is textually implicit (Pearson &

Johnson, 1978) and requires a "read and think about it" answer. Facts and evidence are presented in the reading, but an interpretation must be made. An answer is implied in the reading selection, and the reader must draw a conclusion. What does the author mean? What is the author's purpose? What is the mood of the main character?

*Applied Comprehension:* This is reading beyond the lines (Gray, 1960). The "reader understands unstated relationships between information in text and information in his or her prior knowledge base" (Ruddell, 1997, p. 68).

These levels are not separate or distinct in the process of comprehension. Rather, they occur simultaneously as the reader constructs meaning before, during, and after reading.

Content literacy is the ability to use reading and writing for the acquisition of new content in a given discipline. It is not the same as content knowledge; rather, it represents the skills needed to acquire knowledge of content (McKenna & Robinson, 1997, p. 9). Content literacy strategies facilitate construction of meaning at all levels of comprehension. In order to learn successfully with texts, students must be exposed to a variety of reading and learning strategies that will help them meet the demands of coping with the new vocabulary, concepts, and text organization they will encounter. According to Lapp, Flood, and Farman (1996), three philosophical principles of learning provide the basis for using content literacy instructional strategies:

- Learning occurs most rapidly and efficiently when new concepts and information build on what is already known (Schema Theory).
- The easiest way to gain and hold students' interest and attention is by engaging them in intellectually rich activities that require problem solving, language interactions, and active participation.
- Personal investment in an activity increases and sustains learner persistence and productivity.

**In order to learn successfully with texts, students must be exposed to a variety of reading and learning strategies that will help them meet the demands of coping with the new vocabulary, concepts, and text organization they will encounter.**

There are hundreds of directed reading strategies that promote comprehension and content literacy. Described on the following pages are several strategies that have proven especially beneficial in facilitating student learning. These are active teaching-learning activities that allow students to become involved in, as well as responsible for, their own learning. They require collaboration and, most important, reflective thinking. It is important to match subject matter and content literacy strategy; not all work in every area, although these are nearly global. It's important to know that there are many other strategies available. The content reading textbooks listed in the bibliography for this Professional's Guide are excellent resources.

## Content Literacy Strategies

✦ **GRA** (Group Reading Activity: Manzo, 1990)

This strategy divides responsibility for initial learning and presentation of topic information among several groups in the classroom. The instructor determines the divisions (e.g., in a government unit, the subtopics may be the branches of the government, the amendments to the Constitution, etc.) and assigns a topic and corresponding textbook reading, internet challenge, or research challenge to each group. Groups must determine what is the most important information in the reading, and how that information can best be presented to the rest of the class. Toward the end of the group deliberations, members can visit other groups as critics.

✦ **Jigsaw II** (Slavin, 1994)

Textbook reading is divided by concepts or chapters in a unit. Groups of students become experts on one part of a chapter, a topic, an article, etc. They read it, they discuss their topic, they know the material, they are ready to teach it! Next, groups "Jigsaw" so that they contain an expert from each of the original groups. The new group then works on a common problem, exam questions, essay, class presentation, etc. This is a good way to help students learn the content of a large amount of reading material. Students love this strategy. However, parents may complain IF their students don't "read the entire chapter." The best way to avoid this complaint is to assign the chapter for reading by all and then divide into sections or concepts for intense study.

✦ **Cognitive Mapping/Graphic Organizer**

Learning takes place when new information is integrated into a student's cognitive network, and mapping facilitates this integration with links such as categories, characteristics, and procedures. Maps and graphic organizers can be completed individually, in a cooperative group setting, or as a whole-class activity. They can be used to

- introduce a concept
- connect a concept to a student's frame of reference
- make meaning from text
- review unit concepts
- assess authentically
- study words
- teach each other

Cognitive mapping activities provide learners with an opportunity to collaborate on the construction of a map representing a topic or portion of text under discussion. Just about anything can be the subject of a cognitive map: a chapter, a topic, a literature selection, an experi-

> **Learning takes place when new information is integrated into a student's cognitive network, and mapping facilitates this integration with links such as categories, characteristics, and procedures.**

ment or demonstration, a current event, a newspaper article, a class lecture or discussion, a process, or a description. A map can be a summary activity for an entire unit or a method of organizing text information. Small groups can construct topic maps and share in class presentations via computer, overhead, board, or butcher paper.

Diane Lapp, James Flood, and Nancy Farnan (1996, p. 301) offer this list of frequently used categories of relations to assist in cognitive mapping activities:

| | | |
|---|---|---|
| set/subset | ⇔ | has example/is example of |
| whole/part | ⇔ | has part/is part of |
| characteristics | ⇔ | has characteristic/is characteristic of |
| causal | ⇔ | causes/is caused by |
| spatial/temporal | ⇔ | occurred at/location or time of |

A cognitive map for a history topic is pictured on the next page.

*Discovery of the Americas*

# Columbus, What a Character!

Using the character map below, consider the type of person Columbus was. In the center of the map is the person's name, Christopher Columbus. From that square are four attached circles. In these circles, list four of the most prominent characteristics of Columbus' personality. Then, for each aspect of his personality, use specific examples from the book to support your answer. Write them on the lines attached to the circles.

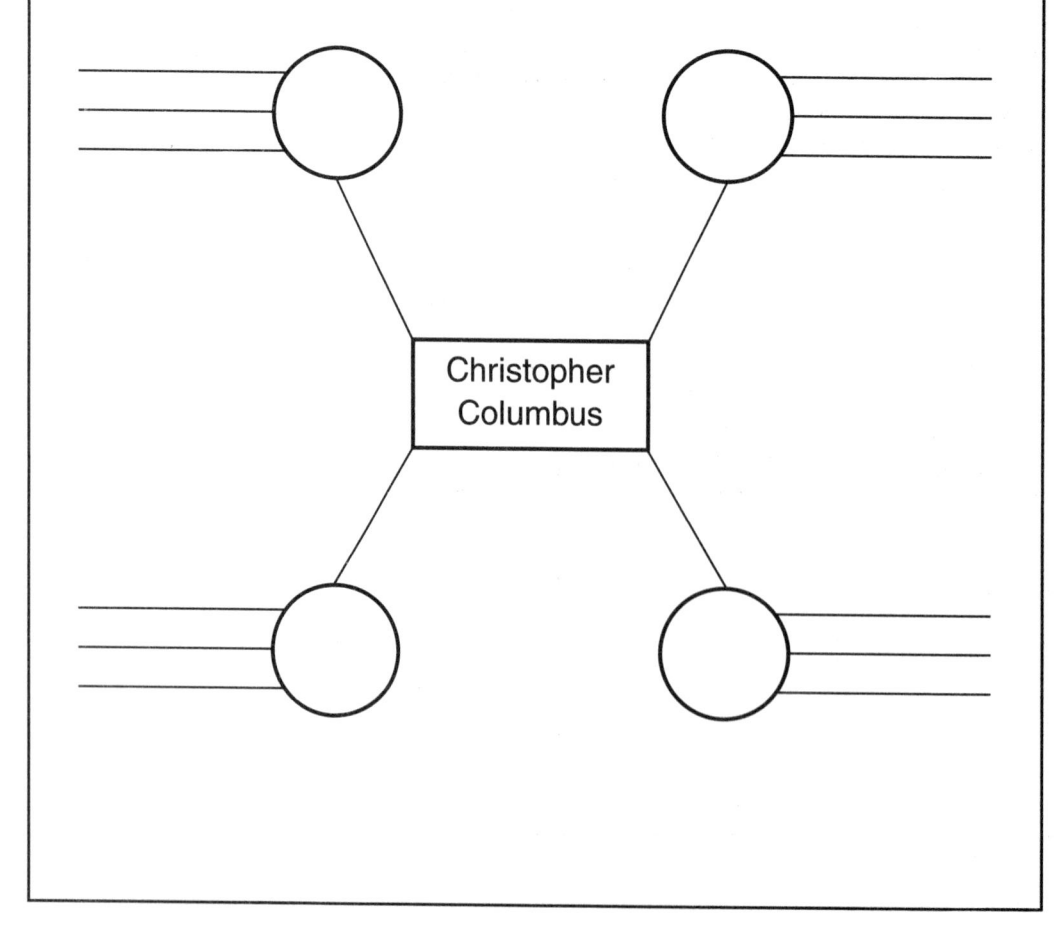

*Reprinted from TCM 472 Learning Through Literature—U.S. History, Teacher Created Materials, Inc., 1994.*

### ✦ Array

This is a very active form of cognitive mapping. Reading material is assigned and a prompt for reading is given ("you will be asked to recall everything you can remember about....you will be asked to describe the process...you will be asked to clarify the concept of..."). Students work in small groups to respond to the prompt by listing important terms, steps, etc. on index cards (or cut pieces of construction paper). Index cards are then "arrayed" on butcher paper in a representation of students' understanding of the concept/reading. The best outcome of this strategy is the group interaction it produces. All students read the same material, but the arrays they produce are usually quite different. Their justification to the large group opens discussion, clarifies concepts, and provides immediate feedback to the instructor.

### ✦ KWL (Ogle, 1986)

In this strategy, teachers elicit from students what they know about a topic and establish with the group a sense of uncertainty about some of their content knowledge that can be turned into questions appropriate to the learning task. First, the teacher engages students in a brainstorming session about the key concepts of a topic to be studied or a chapter to be read. As students share their ideas, usually some disagreements ensue and they begin to question what they "know." From this dialog, the instructor can help students frame questions at points of ambiguity. After this preparation, students read the material and jot down information they learn. When the reading is completed, the class discusses what has been learned, what questions have been answered, and what new questions have been formed.

> The best outcome of this strategy is the group interaction it produces.

| What I KNOW | What I WANT to Learn | What I LEARNED |
|---|---|---|
|  |  |  |
|  |  |  |
|  |  |  |

Additional Comments:

### ✦ Matrix

A matrix shows similarities and differences between two or more things (people, places, events, concepts, processes, etc.). Students work in small groups to read and then compare/contrast target concepts according to attributes, properties, or characteristics.

## Election Facts and Figures

*The Elections*

| | Election of 1960 | Election of 1964 | Election of 1968 |
|---|---|---|---|
| **Democrats** | John F. Kennedy, a senator from Massachusetts, was nominated for president and selected Texas senator Lyndon Baines Johnson as his running mate. | President Lyndon Baines Johnson received the presidential nomination with Minnesota senator Hubert H. Humphrey for vice president. | At a convention marked by protests and violence, Vice President Hubert Humphrey became the presidential candidate with Senator Edmund Muskie of Maine as his running mate. |
| **Republicans** | Vice President Richard M. Nixon ran for president with Henry Cabot Lodge, the U.S. ambassador to the UN, as his vice president. | Barry Goldwater, a conservative senator from Arizona, ran for president with William Miller of New York for vice president. | Former Vice President Richard M. Nixon was paired with Maryland governor Spiro T. Agnew for vice president. |
| **Other** | | | George C. Wallace, former governor of Alabama, broke with the Democrats to form the American Independent Party and ran for president with General Curtis LeMay for vice president. |
| **Issues** | Both candidates had similar political ideas. They believed in a strong military that could protect the United States from a Communist attack and supported funding for welfare programs for the poor. | Goldwater's brand of politics scared many Americans. He opposed civil rights legislation, wanted to make Social Security voluntary, and proposed deep cuts in social programs. | Vietnam remained the big issue in this election. Humphrey found it difficult to distance himself from Johnson, to whom he had remained loyal. Nixon talked vaguely about a secret plan to end the war. Wallace campaigned for strict law and order. |
| **Slogans** | Kennedy promised to lead Americans to a New Frontier. | Johnson's slogan was "All the way with LBJ"; Goldwater's slogan was "In your heart, you know he's right." | |
| **Results** | John F. Kennedy won by a narrow margin—electoral votes, 303 (Kennedy) to 219 (Nixon). Senator Harry F. Byrd received 15 electoral votes. | Johnson won by an overwhelming majority—electoral votes, 486 (Johnson) to 52 (Goldwater). | Nixon received less than 51 percent of the popular vote. The electoral vote was 301 (Nixon) to 191 (Humphrey). Wallace received 45 electoral votes, the strongest third party finish since Theodore Roosevelt in 1912. |

*Reprinted from TCM 2028 The Sixties, Teacher Created Materials, Inc., 1994.*

✦ **Venn Diagram**

A Venn diagram is a summary comparison/contrast organizer that students complete to show individual as well as overlapping characteristics of two concepts. It is particularly useful for concepts that can not be divided exactly because some of their characteristics are quite similar.

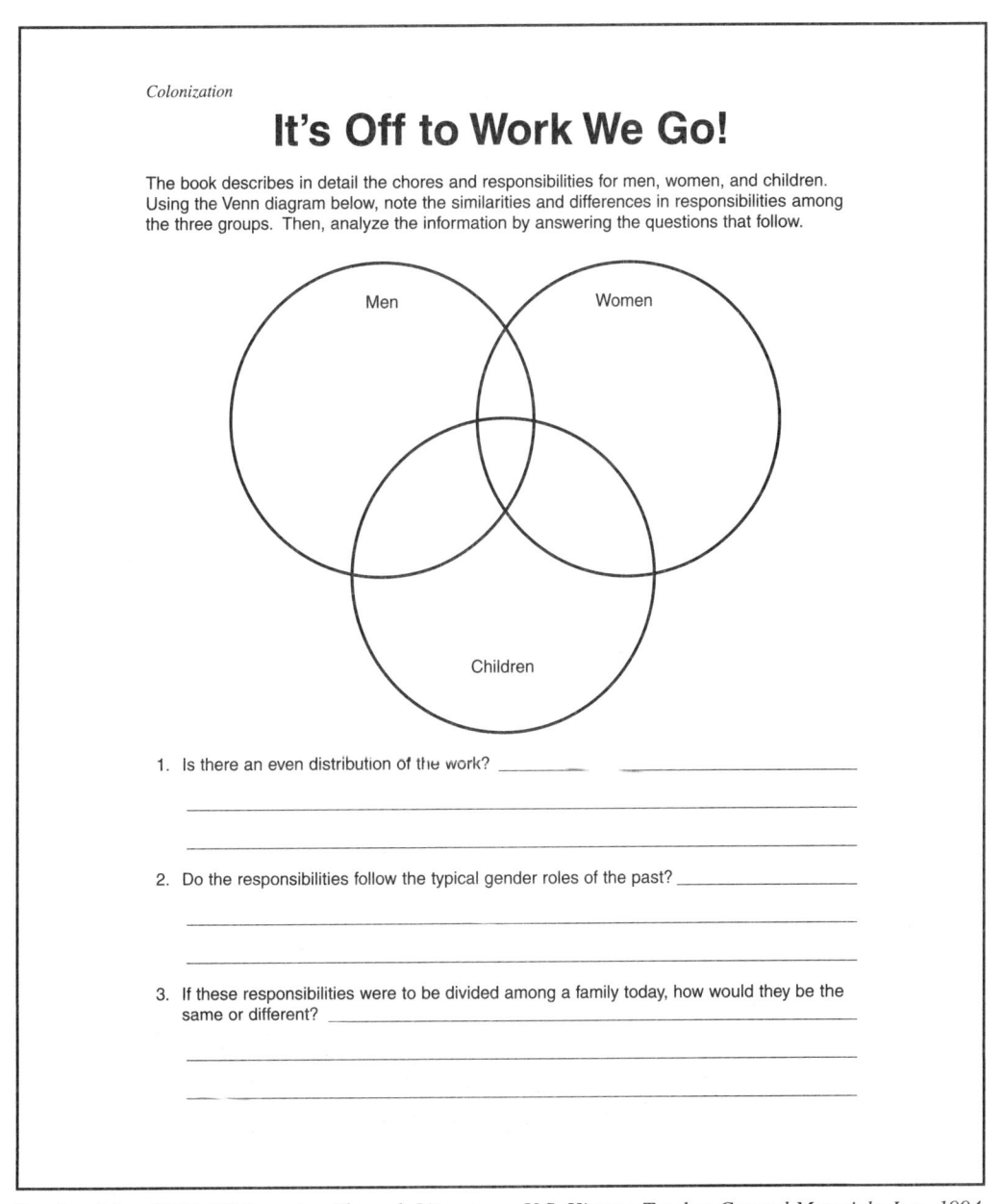

*Colonization*

# It's Off to Work We Go!

The book describes in detail the chores and responsibilities for men, women, and children. Using the Venn diagram below, note the similarities and differences in responsibilities among the three groups. Then, analyze the information by answering the questions that follow.

Men   Women

Children

1. Is there an even distribution of the work? _____

2. Do the responsibilities follow the typical gender roles of the past? _____

3. If these responsibilities were to be divided among a family today, how would they be the same or different? _____

*Reprinted from TCM 472 Learning Through Literature—U.S. History, Teacher Created Materials, Inc., 1994.*

**✦ Cinquain** (Allen & Allen, 1982)

This activity helps students develop the prior knowledge they need for subsequent lessons and provides an opportunity to consolidate, integrate, and synthesize the new information that has been connected with prior knowledge. It is a five-line poem that reflects both affective and cognitive responses to a concept. Responses are often quite amazing. Try it!

> **Line 1** is a one-word title.
> **Line 2** is two words that describe the title.
> **Line 3** is three words expressing an action.
> **Line 4** is four words expressing a feeling.
> **Line 5** is another word for the title.

**✦ Learning Ledger**

A Learning Ledger is a double-entry type journal where each student keeps an account of what he or she knows about the topics of study as well as what is learned. A spiral bound notebook works well. Colored pencils or markers are a must. Students can incorporate content literacy strategies into their ledgers—time lines, T-charts, word webs, etc.

**✦ QAR** (Raphael, 1984)

Students learn to utilize a system of comprehension questions that are categorized according to how and where the answers are located.

- √ *Right There* answers can be found in a single sentence.
- √ *Think and Search* answers require information from several sentences or paragraphs.
- √ *On My Own* answers are generated from the reader's experiences.
- √ *Writer and Me* answers require a coupling of text information and background experiences.

**✦ Organizational Patterns**

"Comprehending explanations in expository material requires a different way of reading than does comprehending stories in narrative material" (Herber & Herber, 1993, p. 229). While narrative material relies on a story line, expository material—text that explains—is organized by relationships that form patterns. Common textbook patterns of organization include listing of information, time order/sequence, comparison/contrast, cause/effect, and definition/example. Students can use transitions—signal words—to help determine the pattern of organization of a selection. In turn, the author's main idea, supporting details, and purpose are easier to ascertain. The following chart clarifies each pattern of organization, provides examples of transitions that signal each pattern, and links subject areas with commonly used patterns.

---

*Sidebar:* **Common textbook patterns of organization include listing of information, time order/sequence, comparison/contrast, cause/effect, and definition/example.**

## Patterns of Organization

| Pattern of Organization | Purpose | Transitions/ Signal Words | Possible Subject Links |
|---|---|---|---|
| Listing | Give facts, details, information (3 reasons, 2 ideas, several points, etc.). | first of all, also, in addition, furthermore, moreover, finally, including | Clothing and package labels<br>Descriptions<br>Safety directions<br>Rules<br>Evidence |
| Time Order | Present information in sequence, order of events or directions (series, stages, dates, etc.). | first, second, third, next, later, before, after, following, last | History time line<br>Instructions to create/do something<br>Procedures<br>Games<br>Science projects<br>Literature plot<br>First aid<br>Word problems<br>Math operations |
| Comparison/Contrast | Show similarities and/or differences. | likewise, however, but, on the other hand, in contrast, similarly, like | Events in history<br>Branches of government<br>Styles of music<br>Art periods<br>Story characters |
| Cause/Effect | What happened? Why did it happen? | because, since, if/then, as a result, therefore | Nutrition<br>Health<br>Events in history<br>Science experiments<br>Sports injuries<br>Sports plays<br>Computer technology |
| Definition/Example | Present a new vocabulary term along with an example of the term. | is/are<br>for example, for instance, such as, to illustrate | Textbooks<br>Technical definitions<br>Specialized word meanings |

## Summary Pyramid (Abbott, 1998)

By following the steps in this guided reading process, readers are facilitated in their efforts to make meaning from text

**Directions:**

1. **Read** the whole story/article/chapter! As you read, underline or highlight important points as well as items that you want to remember.
2. **Complete** the 5W's + 1H Pyramid.
3. **Write** the MAIN IDEA (Who/What + Action).
4. **Write** a SHORT SUMMARY of the reading.
5. **State** the IMPACT: Why is this information important to you?

WHO/What is it about (TOPIC)?

WHAT happened?

WHEN did it take place?

WHERE did it happen?

WHY is it important?  HOW/WHY did it happen?

**Central Point/Main Idea:** (Remember, this must be a complete sentence. It must contain the topic and the most important point about the subject.)

_____
_____
_____

**Summary:**

_____
_____
_____
_____

**Impact:** (Why is this information important?  Be creative.  This is your chance to state your opinion.)

_____
_____
_____
_____

◆ **The Directed Reading-Thinking Activity (DR-TA)** (Stauffer, 1969)

This is an excellent, interest-building strategy that facilitates group comprehension instruction. It is a strategy that can be used with stories or text chapters, and it helps develop higher-level thinking skills. Learners set a purpose for reading, make predictions using their background knowledge, synthesize information, verify and revise predictions as they read, and finally reach independent conclusions about the story or text (Karlsson, 1996, p. 51). The following structured overview describes the steps in the DR-TA:

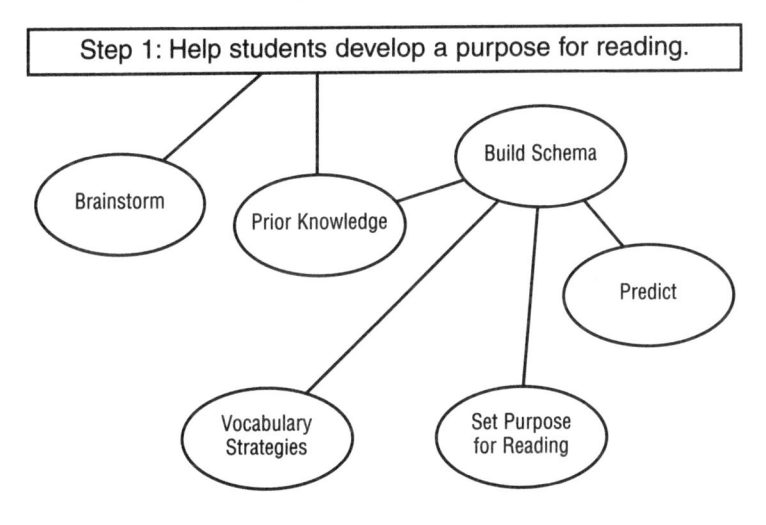

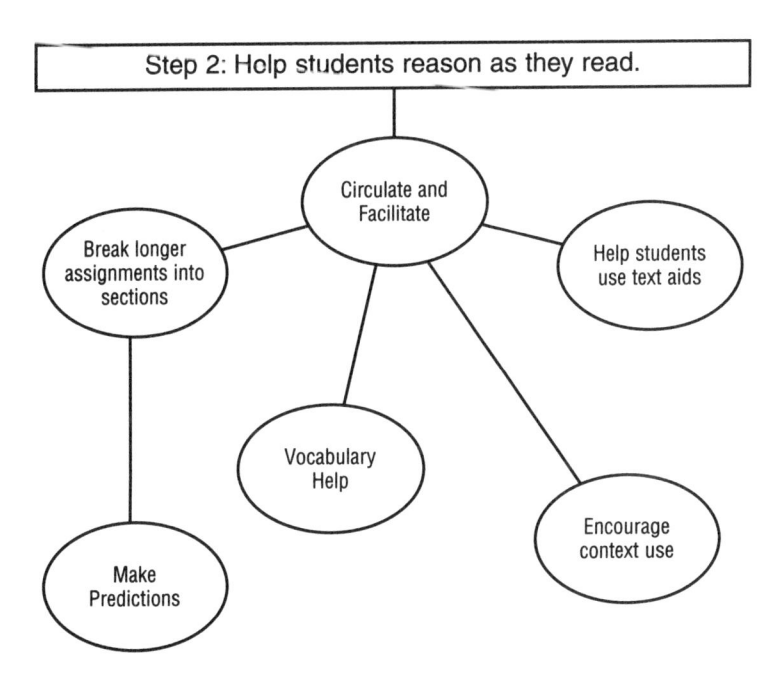

**Step 1: Help students develop a purpose for reading.**
- Brainstorm
- Prior Knowledge
- Build Schema
- Predict
- Vocabulary Strategies
- Set Purpose for Reading

**Step 2: Help students reason as they read.**
- Circulate and Facilitate
- Break longer assignments into sections
- Help students use text aids
- Vocabulary Help
- Encourage context use
- Make Predictions

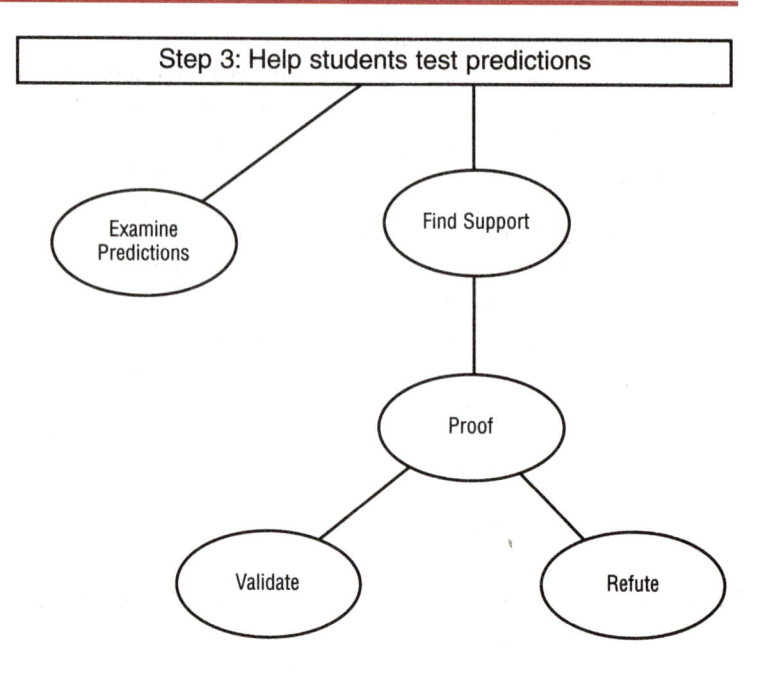

```
Step 3: Help students test predictions
           │
     ┌─────┴─────┐
  Examine      Find Support
 Predictions      │
                Proof
               ┌──┴──┐
           Validate  Refute
```

> **Teachers must use a variety of reading materials to expand student frame of reference and to highlight various styles of writing.**

## Concluding Remarks

Along with content literacy strategies, teachers need to utilize a wide range of subject related materials in the everyday curriculum to ensure that students have ample opportunity to read a variety of materials and build background in a variety of subject areas.

❑ Teachers must use a variety of reading materials to expand student frame of reference and to highlight various styles of writing. These should include the following:
- √ Newspaper articles of various kinds
- √ Functional materials such as job applications, labels, directions for making something or installing something, directions from common cold remedies such as aspirin or cough medicine, and the local bus or train schedule
- √ Literature from various genres including poetry, stories, and essays
- √ Books, books, and more books for a structured, daily leisure reading time
- √ Magazines
- √ Interesting pieces of text from all subject areas

❑ Teachers need to model reading and writing strategies for students. While students read along and listen, the teacher can work through a piece of text to interpret meaning, draw conclusions, and make judgments. The teacher should also point out transitions—words like *also, in addition, on the other hand, because, instead, for example*—and show how they connect sentences or paragraphs and develop relationships. Students should practice these skills in cooperative groups or "teach" a passage to the their classmates. Students should learn to recognize patterns of paragraph organization— listing, cause and effect, comparison and contrast, definition and example, time order or sequence—to enhance ability to analyze, synthesize, and make applications.

❑ Teachers should have students write, write, and write some more! Writing is a way of knowing, a way of thinking, a way of exploring. Students need to practice writing to prompts of various domains. They can write a letter that is persuasive, explore a controversial topic, evaluate a piece of literature or a television program, or tell a story. Prewriting strategies such as brainstorming or clustering should be taught. Journal writing as a daily activity should be encouraged.

By promoting content literacy strategies, teachers add tools to their repertoire that shift the educational focus from teaching to learning, from passive acquisition of facts and routines to the active application of ideas to problems. By placing students in collaborative problem-solving groups and providing reading assignments that require analysis and creativity, higher order cognitive skills can be developed.

Content literacy strategies help the underprepared student as well as the gifted. They are vital for students whose basic skills are weak and those who speak English as a second language because they offer opportunities to clarify concepts and receive help with technical and specialized vocabulary. In addition, students with higher literacy skills are provided a chance to teach, commonly acknowledged as the best way to learn a subject!

> **By placing students in collaborative problem-solving groups and providing reading assignments that require analysis and creativity, higher order cognitive skills can be developed.**

# Creating Readers: Motivating Students to READ!

**All students need to develop the motivation to read for pleasure as well as for purpose.**

The paradigm described in Chapter 1 describes a need to create independent readers. All students need to develop the motivation to read for pleasure as well as for purpose. I give an assignment to my university graduates to write a paper entitled *Me...A Reader!* They are asked to describe what they remember about the process of learning to read as well as where they are as readers today. Nearly all of them remember something about learning to read—a favorite teacher, Mark and Janet, Dick and Jane, instruction in phonics, or storytime with mom, dad, or grandma. Some of them even remember favorite books: *Amelia Bedelia, Curious George* (remember the man in the yellow hat?), and *Bunicula,* to name a few. What most of these students have in common, though, is recalling that they seldom read anything but what was required—textbooks and classics—in middle grades and beyond. One future teacher went so far as to change the title of the assignment to *Me...A Reader, NOT!* The sad fact is that many adults, including teachers, do not read for pleasure, and they haven't since elementary school. Perhaps the starting point for motivating students to read is to first motivate teachers as well as parents to do so. Parents and teachers are the best "reader role models" that students can possible have.

## Leisure Reading

One of the best ways to motivate students to read is to initiate a leisure reading program—either in individual classes or schoolwide.

Set aside a daily period of time where *everyone* reads. If this becomes a schoolwide initiative, "everyone" means just that—students, teachers, principal, administrative staff, classified staff, and any parents, visitors, or vendors who happen to be on campus during leisure reading time! Remember that a leisure reading program belongs in every classroom, not just the English classroom! The following guidelines for establishing a successful leisure reading program are based on the teachings of Dr. Harold Graham, Professor Emeritus, California State University, Long Beach.

> **Remember that a leisure reading program belongs in every classroom, not just the English classroom!**

### Things to Do

✳ Provide books on a wide variety of subjects that relate to students' needs and interests. (Paperbacks are preferable.) Students can bring their own books but don't require it. Have many, many good books available for their choosing.

✳ Books should be on many different reading levels. Include many high interest, "easy read" books.

✳ Provide a specific period of class time—daily is preferred. A ten to fifteen minute period at the beginning of class works best.

✳ Have students keep a record of books read, simply by author and title.

✳ Display books around the room.

✳ Encourage students (as well as the teachers) to join a book club—TAB (Scholastic) is great!

✳ Display new books as often as possible.

✳ Keep a regular reading habit along with the students. Read while they are reading.

✳ Let students select the books they wish to read.

✳ Confer with students about the books they are reading.

✳ Frequently encourage students to share comments about the books they are reading.

**Things Not to Do**

* Do not require written book reports.
* Do not give points for books read.
* Do not force students to read aloud in front of the class.
* Do not use the term "Free Reading," its connotation is too close to "free time."
* Do not insist on stressing the "classics."
* Do not grade students on the number of books or pages they have read.
* Do not rule out a book because it has a small number of pages.
* Do not rule out a book because it has been a movie.
* Do not force students to finish books they do not like.

**How to Start**

There are many inexpensive ways to get books to initiate or expand a leisure reading program.

* Ask the parent-teacher organization to sponsor a book drive.
* Ask a local book retailer to help organize a book sale.
* Ask a local retailer to post a flyer "We need books… ," or set out a collection basket.
* Post a flyer during end-of-year locker clean out time at the local high school.
* Get your students to participate in a book club and use the reward points to get free books and posters for the classroom.
* Visit garage sales.

## Create a Reading Environment

The classroom environment should entice and encourage students to read. Paperback books, a variety of magazines, and daily newspapers should be in proud disarray because they are utilized in every classroom. The American Library Association is an excellent resource for posters, bookmarks, and other reading incentives. Visit their Web site at: *http://www.ala.org/*

Classroom reading materials and incentives can be general or subject specific. Bulletin boards and learning centers are also great mediums for incorporating reading beyond the textbook. Bulletin boards catch attention and motivate students to learn more by reading. Learning centers offer an active teaching-learning environment for reading that can "provide children with endless opportunities to explore concepts in a variety of ways" (McClay, 1996, p. 1).

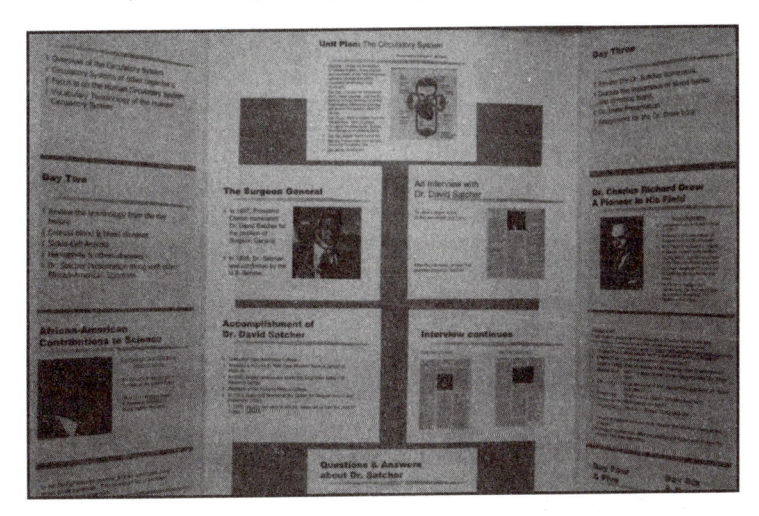

**The classroom environment should entice and encourage students to read.**

**Interactive Learning Center**

**Interactive
Bulletin
Boards**

## Creating Partnerships: Home and Community

In *Encouraging Your Junior High Student to Read,* John Shefelbine gives advice to parents about the importance of reading for junior high age children:

√ Practice Makes Perfect

√ Wide Reading Contributes to Success in School

√ Reading Facilitates Personal Growth and Enjoyment

According to Shefelbine, good readers practice reading—they read outside school and beyond class assignments (1991, p. 9). The pamphlet entitled *You Can Encourage Your High School Student to Read* offers this good advice to parents: do not tell kids to read because it's good for them; rather, let them see how reading serves their own needs. Parents should let their children see them using reading materials to find information as well as reading for pleasure. They need to talk about reading with their children, and they need to provide a variety of reading materials at home (Myers, 1991, p. 6).

Try Choices to get community members involved in schoolwide pleasure reading initiatives. Invite community members, role models, to present an informal "book talk" with a class or for an assembly. Have the speaker bring his or her "choice," all-time favorite book, to share. The pool of potential speakers is unlimited; book talk presenters for my students have included a college president, a Superior Court judge, and a member of the school board. Community members love to participate, and students love to see and hear about Choices, which have included Dr. Seuss, *Where the Red Fern Grows,* and an economics textbook!

> Invite community members, role models, to present an informal "book talk" with a class or for an assembly.

Selections presented during Choices can then be displayed in the library or administration building lobby for students and visitors to see.

## Finding the Right Books

Walk through any major bookstore and take a look at the adolescent fiction section–it is almost an overwhelming experience. There are so many books to choose from. If in doubt about books to select, start with a book club newsletter (such as Scholastic's TAB), as these usually have current "hot picks." Also, browse internet sights such as *www.amazon.com*; categories to search include children's books or young adult selections. Here you will find information about young adult current best selling books as well as classics. Book topics include adventures and thrillers, teen issues (nonfiction), love and romance, and sports. Book reviews are included, many written by the young people who have purchased copies.

A second source is a published book list. There are many available, and favorites include those found on the Web site for the American Library Association. These Young Adult Library Service Association (YALSA) lists include Best Books for Young Adults, Quick Picks for Young Adults, Popular Paperbacks for Young Adults, and Top 10 Best Books for Young Adults. The International Reading Association publishes the following books that are helpful in choosing classroom reading material: *Nonfiction for the Classroom* by Milton Meltzer, *More Teens' Favorite Books,* and *Magazines for Kids and Teens.* They also publish the following lists that are available in large quantities for a reasonable price: Children's Choices, Teachers' Choices, and Young Adults' Choices.

## Read Aloud to Students

**Read something to students every day.**

Read something to students every day. Read anything and everything—from a snippet to an entire book. Read the newspaper, a children's book, one of Aesop's Fables, an urban legend, a famous quote, a fact, a joke, or a brainteaser. Read something that grabs attention, touches an emotion, informs, entertains, or motivates. Vary the type of reading from day to day; the only requirement is that it must be interesting.

## Read Aloud Resources

Canfield, Jack, et.al.
  *Chicken Soup for the Teenage Soul: 101 Stories of Life and Love.* Health Communications, 1996.
  *Chicken Soup for the Soul.* Health Communications, 1996.

Davis, Kenneth C.
  *Don't Know Much About Geography: Everything You Need to Know About Geography But Never Learned.* Avon Books, 1995.
  *Don't Know Much About History: Everything You Need to Know About American History But Never Learned.* Avon Books, 1991.

Lederer, Richard.
  *Anguished English.* Laureleaf, 1989.
  *Get Thee to a Punnery.* Laureleaf, 1995.

Scieszka, Jon and Lane Smith.
  *The True Story of the Three Little Pigs.* Puffin, 1996.
  *Squids will be Squids.* Viking, 1998.

Silverstein, Shel.
  *Where the Sidewalk Ends.* Harper Collins, 1974.

Steptoe, John L., and Clarita Kohen.
  *Mufaro's Beautiful Daughters: An African Tale.* Lothrop. Lee, & Shepard, 1987.

Trelease, Jim.

*The Read Aloud Handbook,* 4th Edition. Penguin USA, 1995.
*Hey! Listen to This: Stories to Read Aloud.* Penguin USA, 1992.

Wood, Douglas, and Cheng-Khee Chee.

*Old Turtle.* Pfeifer-Hamilton Publisher, 1992.

Young, Mark, Ed.

*The Guinness Book of World Records.* Bantam Books, 1998.

## Concluding Remarks

Reading plays a particularly significant role for young people between the ages of 10 and 14. Students in this age range find themselves in a developmental stage where profound physical, cognitive, and social changes are occurring as they mature. Reading can help adolescents explore their interests, develop social and cognitive skills, work through problems, and build positive self-esteem.

Students need encouragement and active support from school, family, and community to ensure they become avid readers. Teachers need to provide time, motivation, and resources for reading; they must be role models by sharing their interest and value for reading.

> *One of the attributes of mentors and influential teachers is that they transform students from people who "study math" (or any other subject) to people who "Do math" (or any other subject), and Doing math or science or literature or football means one reads and writes in that area for the rest of his or her life, regardless of whether that lifelong involvement is part of a career choice (Ruddell, 1997, p. 367).*

Students are most likely to become readers if they see their parents, teachers, and other adults using reading to find information as well as enjoying reading as a pleasure activity.

---

**Recipe for a Reader**

1   Teacher, parent, or adult who loves to read
1   Large bowl of popcorn
1   Favorite book
1   Special time set-aside just for reading

Mix with read-aloud roles for everyone, a little laughter, a pinch of sadness, and heaps of inspiration.

(*Hint:* recipe works best with a cold television!)

---

**Reading can help adolescents explore their interests, develop social and cognitive skills, work through problems, and build positive self-esteem.**

# References

Abbott, S. (1997). Professional's guide: Standardized testing. Westminster, CA: Teacher Created Materials, Inc.

Allen, R. & Allen, C. (1982). Language experience activities (2nd ed.). Boston, MA: Houghton Mifflin.

Alverman, D. & Phelps, S. (1998). Content reading and literacy: Succeeding in today's diverse classrooms. Needham Heights: MA: Allyn and Bacon.

Anderson, R.C., Hilbert, E.H., Scott, J.A. & Wilkinson, I. (Eds.). (1985). Becoming a nation of readers: The report of the Commission on Reading. Washington, DC: National Institute of Education.

Anderson, R.C. (1993). In Harris, T., Hodges, R. (Eds.), The literacy dictionary: The vocabulary of reading and writing. Newark, DE: International Reading Association.

Armento, B., Nash, G., Salter, C. & Wixson, K. (1991). A message of ancient days: Houghton Mifflin social studies. Boston, MA: Houghton Mifflin.

Badger, E. (1992). Open-ended questions in reading (ERIC/TM Digest). Washington, DC: ERIC Clearinghouse on Tests, Measurement, and Evaluation. ERIC Document Reproduction Service No. ED 355 253)

Fry, E. (1977). Fry's readability graph: clarifications, validity, and extension to level 17. Journal of Reading, 21, 242-252.

Gray, W. (1960). The major aspects of reading. In H. Robinson (Ed.) Development of reading abilities. Supplementary Educational Monograph, 90. Chicago, ILL: University of Chicago Press.

Harris, T.L. & Hodges, R.E. (Eds.). (1995). The literacy dictionary: The vocabulary of reading and writing. Newark, DE: International Reading Association.

Herber, H.L. (1978). Teaching reading in the content areas (2nd ed.). Englewood Cliffs, NJ: Prentice Hall.

Herber, H.L. & Herber, J.N. (1993). Teaching in content areas with reading, writing, and reasoning. Needham Heights, MA: Allyn & Bacon.

Karlsson, M. R. (1996). Professional's guide: Motivating at-risk students. Westminster, CA: Teacher Created Materials, Inc.

Lapp, D., Flood, J. & Farnan, N. (1996). Content area reading and learning instructional strategies (2nd ed.). Needham Heights, Massachusetts: Allyn & Bacon.

Love, D. (1998, August 30). Move to middle school tumultuous for kids, parents. The Orange County Register, Back to School'98, p. 7

Mack, A. (1998, July 23) Fighting the high school rule of 55. The Los Angeles Times, p. B13.

Manzo, A. & Manzo, U. (1990). Content area reading: A heuristic approach. Columbus, OH: Merrill.

McClay, J.M. (1996). Professional's guide: Learning centers. Westminster, CA: Teacher Created Materials, Inc.

McKenna, M. C. & Robinson, R.D. (1997). Teaching through text (2nd ed.). White Plains, NY: Longman Publishers.

Myers, J. (1990). You can encourage your high school student to read. Newark, DE: International Reading Association.

Ogle, D. (1986). K-W-L: A literacy model that develops active reading of expository text. The Reading Teacher, 39, 564-570.

Pearson, P. D. & Johnson, D. D. (1978). Teaching reading comprehension. New York: Holt, Rinehart, and Winston.

Raphael, T. (1984). Teaching learners about sources of information for answering comprehension questions. Journal of Reading, 28, 303-311.

Roe, B. D., Stoodt, B. D., & Burns, P.C. (1991). Secondary school reading instruction: The content areas (4th ed.). Boston, MA: Houghton Mifflin Company.

Ruddell, M. R. (1997). Teaching content reading and writing (2nd ed.). Needham heights, MA: Allyn & Bacon.

Ryan, C. D. (1994). Professional's guide: Authentic assessment. Westminster, CA: Teacher Created Materials, Inc.

Ryder, R. J. & Graves, M. F. (1998). Reading and learning in content areas (2nd ed.). Upper Saddle River, NJ: Merrill.

Shefelbine, J. (1991). Encouraging your junior high student to read. Newark, DE: International Reading Association.

Slavin, R. (1994). Using student team learning (4th ed.). Baltimore, MD: John Hopkins University Center for Social Organization of Schools.

Smith, C. F. & Kepner, H. S. (1981). Reading in the mathematics classroom. Washington, D.C.: National Education Association.

Stauffer, R. (1969). Directing reading maturity as a cognitive process. New York: Harper and Row.

Thelen, J. (1976). Improving reading in science. Newark, DE: International Reading Association.

Vacca, R. & Vacca, J. A. (1996). Content area reading (5th ed.). New York: Harper Collins College Publishers.

Walley, C. & Walley, K. (1995). Integrating literature in content areas. Westminster, CA: Teacher Created Materials, Inc.

Williams, P.L., Reese, C.M., Campbell, J.R., Mazzeo, J., & Phillips, G.W. (1995). National assessment of educational progress, reading: A First Look, Revised edition. Washington, D.C.: U.S. Department of Education, Office of Educational Research and Improvement.

## Teacher Created Materials Resource List

TCM 169 Maps, Charts, Graphs & Diagrams (Intermediate)

TCM 194 Middle School Study Skills

TCM 400 Literature Unit: Wilson Rawl's <u>Where the Red Fern Grows</u>

TCM 472 Learning Through Literature: U.S. History (Intermediate)

TCM 492 Focus on Composers (Grades 4-8)

TCM 494 Focus on Artists (Grades 4-8)

TCM 499 Focus on Athletes (Grades 4-8)

TCM 652 Activities for Language Arts (Challenging)

TCM 658 Activities for Math (Challenging)

TCM 781 Language Arts Assessment (Grades 5-6)

TCM 838 Professional's Guide: Authentic Assessment

TCM 843 Professional's Guide: Integrating Literature in Content Areas

TCM 890 Professional's Guide: Motivating At-Risk Students

TCM 891 Professional's Guide: Learning Centers

TCM 2028 The Sixties (Challenging)

TCM 2124 Professional's Guide: Standardized Testing